Grandma's Wartime Kitchen

ALSO BY JOANNE LAMB HAYES
(with Bonnie Tandy Leblang)

Grains
Beans
365 Great Cookies and Brownies
Rice
Country Entertaining
The Weekend Kitchen

Grandma's Wartime Kitchen

WORLD WAR II AND THE WAY WE COOKED

Joanne Lamb Hayes

ST. MARTIN'S PRESS ❧ NEW YORK

IN MEMORY OF

MY FATHER, LEROY DAVIS LAMB, AND

MY AUNT AND UNCLE, CATHERINE LEESE PETTY

AND PAUL PETTY

www.stmartins.com

Book design by Victoria Kuskowski

Library of Congress Cataloging-in-Publication Data

Hayes, Joanne Lamb.
   Grandma's wartime kitchen: World War II and the way we cooked /
Joanne Lamb Hayes.
      p. cm.
   Includes bibliographical references and index.
   ISBN 0-312-25323-0
   1. Cookery, American—History—20th century. 2. World War, 1939–
1945—Food supply—United States. I. Title.
TX715.H3937 2000
641.5973'09'004—dc21

00–031812

10 9 8 7 6 5 4

Contents

Acknowledgments

MY THANKS TO: Dorothy Leese Lamb, my mother, for filling my childhood with opportunity despite the restrictions of wartime and for remembering in detail and sharing with me her home-front experiences. She has been the inspiration for this book, as for most I do.

Heather and Claire Hayes, my daughters, who carried home the groceries, tested when I tired, kept my computer happy, and along with their friends Jonathan Nanberg and Tyson Lewis served as a gracious and positive taste panel. The book would not have been possible without their help and support!

Hilda Lanhardt Hayes, the world's best mother-in-law, for her continued friendship and for saving her ration books.

Angela Miller, my agent, for her confidence in the book and for finding it the perfect home.

Jean Anderson, for always knowing the answer to my questions, for her many wonderful stories of the early forties, and for writing the Foreword to this book.

Marian Lizzi, my editor, and the staff at St. Martin's Press for cheerfully and efficiently nurturing the book through production.

Jenene Garey, Philip Hosay, and Christine Nystrom, my dissertation committee at New York University, for their guidance while I was doing the research that led to my Ph.D. dissertation and eventually to this book.

Marion Nestle, chairman of the New York University Department of Nutrition and Food Studies, for her encouragement while I was working on the project and for creating a department in which food history research is possible.

Jan Longone of the Wine and Food Library in Ann Arbor, Michigan, for generously giving her time and resources when I had questions.

Amy Bentley, assistant professor of Nutrition and Food Studies, for sharing her research on the World War II home front.

Mabel Chan, Gordon M. Pradl, Judith Weissman, and Margret Wolf for their insightful questions as members of my orals committees.

The more than 300 home-front cooks who wrote to me in 1991 when I first started research on this subject.

Foreword

With the arrival of a new century and a new millennium, it's hardly surprising that several cookbooks have surfaced to trace our culinary journey through the twentieth century. What is surprising is the scant attention they pay to World War II and its impact upon the way we ate and the way we cooked even though that impact is still felt today.

With *Grandma's Wartime Kitchen: World War II and the Way We Cooked*, Joanne Lamb Hayes amply fills the void. Her coverage of the forties—the war decade—is painstakingly researched yet fascinating to read, thanks to her own childhood memories plus those of countless moms across the country who coped and cooked in those lean days of food rationing.

I was a little girl when World War II broke out and so many of the things my own mother did to stretch meat and salve her family's sweet tooth despite strict sugar rationing sprang to mind as I read *Grandma's Wartime Kitchen*. I'm grateful to Joanne Lamb Hayes for explaining what I was too young to understand at the time (and didn't bother to learn later). Why, for example, did roast chicken, fricasseed rabbit, and braised beef heart replace prime ribs and roast leg of lamb as the traditional centerpieces of our Sunday dinners? (*Because poultry and game weren't rationed and lesser cuts of meat required fewer points.*) Why did so many of our desserts begin with a can of purple plums? (*The heavy syrup in which they were packed could be used as a sweetener.*) Why did our home-made ice creams always contain sweetened condensed milk? (*It was an effective sweetener.*) And why was the margarine we used in place of butter white? (*Dairy farmers, a powerful voice even then, insisted that yellow margarine not be sold.*) The brand Mother bought came with a little capsule of orange dye and my job was to knead it in slowly, thoroughly, so that the white blob turned a bright buttery hue. Not easy even though the kneading could be done right in the unopened cellophane package.

The book's discussion of Victory Gardens reminded me of my own family's war effort, which included not only a vegetable garden and strawberry patch but also chickens for eggs and for eating. I'll never forget the day Daddy brought home a cardboard box filled with cheeping balls of fluff. Or helping him improvise a basement pen of boards, then adding low-wattage lightbulbs to keep the baby chicks warm.

When the birds graduated to the backyard, it was my chore to feed them, gather eggs, and—I still shudder to think—pluck and eviscerate the over-the-hill hens that my father killed. Hardly child's play. These tough old birds would be simmered into soups and stews. Or just cooked until so tender so that the meat could be stripped from the bones, then slipped into sandwiches, salads, and casseroles.

The "Cultivate and Can" chapter spun me back to the canning marathons that took place every summer in my mother's kitchen. The whole family would pitch in, and to keep my brother and me interested, my parents turned the tomato peeling, bean snapping, and corn husking into a competition. (If memory serves, the fastest peeler/snapper/husker got a dollar.) Platoons of canning jars stood at the ready as did Mother's pressure canner, a jiggling, steam-spewing monster that terrified me.

Mother's mantra in those war years: "Eat your vegetables…eat your vegetables…eat your vegetables." And Daddy's: "Eat your carrots, they'll make your eyes bright." Both, no doubt, were steeped in the cheery snippets of "victory advice" dished out by the leading magazines of the day, the major food companies, and not least, the United States government. *Grandma's Wartime Kitchen* includes scores of these: "Your first job in wartime is to feed your family well"; "Eat the Right Food, U.S. Needs US strong"; "Vitamins Vital for Victory."

Grandma's Wartime Kitchen is a valuable resource that shows us how inventive our mothers and grandmothers were at coping with World War II rationing of meat, sugar, butter, cheese, and a staggering array of canned foods, often while holding jobs outside the home. And this, mind you, without electric dishwashers and all the other labor-saving appliances we take for granted today.

Particularly touching is the quote on page 63 from a woman who came home from work dead tired, put a proper meal on the table for her children, then stayed up half the night canning produce from her Victory Garden. Sad to say, she, along with millions of other patriotic women, were fired at the war's end to make room for the returning soldiers. How many of us knew *that*?

If only for its in-depth documentation of the 1940s, *Grandma's Wartime Kitchen* is a welcome addition to twentieth-century American literature. But it is a cookbook, too, a splendid one that serves up a memorable collection of forties recipes, the quick and easy "comfort foods" so many of us crave today in this age of show-off chefs: meat loaves (some with soy flour added to pump up the protein), ham and egg pie, chicken and waffles, corn fritters, potato rolls, winter squash biscuits, raised chocolate cake, whipped cream cake, Dutch apple cake—plus a fascinating group of frugal recipes showing how to trim precious sugar and butter by using cake, cookie, and cracker crumbs.

Grandma's Wartime Kitchen includes so many of the recipes I remember my mother making that to curl up with it is like taking a trip home. For me, no other book so effectively recaptures the scents, the sights, and the sounds of my youth.

And no other book gives the 1940s their proper place in our culinary history.

Jean Anderson, author of THE AMERICAN CENTURY COOKBOOK

Introduction

Several years ago, as we were celebrating the fiftieth anniversary of the end of World War II, I attended a seminar on American eating habits. The keynote speaker awakened the audience by saying "when Japan bombed Pearl Harbor, American women left the kitchen and never returned." I knew she was wrong. Although I wasn't very old on December 7, 1941, most of my time was spent in the kitchen and I remembered things being pretty busy there. I was determined to find the truth about women in wartime America. As I thought about all the good things that came from that kitchen, I got hungrier and hungrier. But where were those recipes? Long replaced in my mother's recipe book by "more up-to-date things," those fresh, frugal, from-scratch recipes for which I hungered had to be around somewhere. Thus started a quest through libraries, used-book and -magazine stores, and yard sales that filled my living room with piles of yellowing printed material and my kitchen with delicious memories. As I was reading the cookbooks, magazine food articles, and consumer pamphlets, I felt that I was given the opportunity to peek into a 1940s icebox or "mechanical" refrigerator. What was inside not only gave clues to the tastes of the times but to the ingenuity of the American homemaker when faced with a unique set of circumstances.

In addition to finding the recipes I remembered, I discovered a lot about the women who created them. Did they leave the home? Yes, when the government asked for their help, they responded immediately. All over the country, women followed the example of Rosie the Riveter and Wendy the Welder. Some learned to do jobs formerly done by men, others became clerical workers or Red Cross volunteers, and many ran family farms. According to Mintz and Kellogg in *Domestic Revolutions: A Social History of American Family Life*, the number of women in the labor force soared from 14 to 19 million. Nearly half of all American women held a job at some point during the war. While in peacetime, employed women were mostly young and unmarried, during the war three quarters of the women entering the work force were married.

But did they leave their kitchens? Only for a part of their day. Not only were they not given permission to ease up on kitchen standards because of all the extra responsibilities they had taken on, but the media continued to emphasize the importance of providing hearty menus, setting an attractive table, and appearing perfectly attired and coifed for the dinner hour. In essence, women were asked to work harder and harder, and they rose to the challenge.

As long as mostly regular Army and young single enlistees left for Europe, a woman's role was still clearly that of homemaker. In 1942, magazines told homemakers "your first job in wartime is to feed your family well," "our home front lies in the kitchens of America," "American housewives are responsible for keeping eighteen times as many men properly fed on the Production Front as those who feed the men on the Fighting Front." Women were reminded that "There's a War Job in every kitchen" and were addressed as "the first home guard" and "soldiers in house dresses." But by 1943, the message to women was to get a job. Government-sponsored ads clearly stated, "The more women at work, the sooner we'll win," "your country needs you in a vital job," and "harness that housework energy and skill to any home front service." Persuasion took many different forms. A well-dressed model in a fashion article advised readers, "This is the way I look for a job," while a uniformed WAC quipped, "I'd rather be with them than waiting for them."

Although the media continued to support women's wartime roles through the summer of 1945, they gradually began to construct the foundations for a very different postwar lifestyle. For most women there was no decision: The day the war ended thousands of them all over America were fired to make jobs available for returning soldiers. As their world shrank back to the home, women continued to garden and can as they had during the war. However, many of the delicious dishes made with alternative wartime ingredients became memories as new supermarkets became filled with frozen, dehydrated, and packaged products.

There is no question in my mind that the memory of those three years, eight months, and seven days has dominated all else that has happened to America in this century. The men and women who pulled together "for the duration" came out of the experience with the confidence and energy to build a dynamic nation. And even today, if you get several of them together in a room the conversation sooner or later turns to "The War." In 1941, I was too young to know exactly what was happening and to know that things weren't always going to be that way, but I remember the blackouts, standing in line for ration books, boarders living in our extra room, and the shelves of beautifully canned fruit and vegetables in our basement. I was never hungry—I don't think many Americans were—

but we were all reminded that our Allies in Europe needed a share of our bounty because the war had destroyed their farms and factories. The most exciting evening of my young life was the night in August of 1945 when the lights came on at the movie theater in our small town. The whole town came out to see it.

In collecting the recipes for this book, I spoke to women who had cooked for their families during those trying times. They were unanimous in their feeling of pride in their contribution to the cause and their certainty that there was not really a lack of food, just not always the kind of food you really wanted. Many look back to the thriftiness they had learned during the First World War and the Depression to come up with creative ways to cope with the shortages. Surprisingly, many of those techniques and the dishes they are associated with have come to represent comfort to us today. Rather than reminding us of a time when a threatening world made it necessary for us to raise and preserve our own fruits and vegetables and eat lots of meat loaf so a half pound of beef would serve six, they remind us of the security of Grandma's kitchen and the delicious foods that came from it. The pages that follow are filled with those memories, translated and tested for today's kitchens, but still just as delicious, nourishing, and time saving as they were fifty years ago.

In addition, you will find an occasional "Wartime Special" recipe, printed just the way it was published during the war. These recipes are so much a part of their time that you probably won't want to serve them today, but they are an interesting record of the ways in which people coped and I found them lots of fun to read.

THE HOME-FRONT WARRIOR

★ ★ ★ ★ ★ ★ ★ ★ ★ ★ ★ ★ ★ ★ ★ ★ ★ ★ ★ ★

Cream of Onion Soup

Ladies Aid Salad

Star Salad

Watercress and Grapefruit Salad

White House Salad

Monday Meat Loaf

Pork Shoulder Roast with Stuffed Onions

Sausage Link Loaf

Swedish Meat Balls

Squash Biscuits

Whole Wheat Bread

Butterscotch Pie

Cottage Pudding with Toffee Sauce

Plum Tarts

Salvage Pudding

EVER BAKE A CAKE WITH A CANDLE?

1 IT CAN BE DONE—with a Wear-Ever pan! Not that we advise it for daily use, with your kitchen range so much more convenient . . . but this amazing test shows how evenly heat spreads throughout all Wear-Ever utensils.

Actual photograph, un-retouched

2 EVENLY BAKED, isn't it—all through!—though from one tiny candle flame! That's because in Wear-Ever Aluminum, the *whole pan cooks the food!* This means happier results in *all kinds* of cooking, avoiding hot spots and scorching.

The June 1942 issue of *Good Housekeeping* announced that the magazine had been asked to plan the menus and market orders for feeding 450 airmen stationed in the Middle East. This is their suggested market order for a year:

Strawberry jam	12,000 pounds
Canned grapefruit	225 dozen #110 cans
Macaroni	2,025 pounds
String beans	1,013 dozen #2 cans
Powdered milk	4,798 pounds
Coffee	7,500 pounds
Flour	73,881 pounds
Vanilla	140 gallons
Dried beans	4,320 pounds
Shortening	30,000 pounds
Molasses	15 dozen #10 cans
Cookies	4,000 pounds
Canned hams	24,300 pounds

The period between December 7, 1941 (the bombing of Pearl Harbor), and August 14, 1945 (Japan's surrender), was a time of dramatic changes in the lives of American women. After the years of the Great Depression, in which working-class women were mostly employed in menial jobs and middle-class women stayed at home, the U.S. government suddenly encouraged all women to enter the wartime workforce, respond to wartime programs such as rationing and victory gardening, and volunteer for Red Cross work, war bond drives, civil defense posts, and community activities. When women's roles were extended to include these activities, their food-, nutrition-, and health-related responsibilities were elevated to the level of patriotism. As the male population disappeared into the armed services, the nation asked more and more of the American homemaker. The government produced, and encouraged businesses to sponsor, pamphlets, articles, and posters that gave the home-front housewife all the advice she needed to work a ten-hour defense-plant shift, come home to serve a nutritious meal on an impeccably set table for her family, have the kitchen spotless in no time, and in the morning, look absolutely perky as she handed each family member a hearty lunch before she started the next long day. In season, planting, harvesting, and preserving added to the daily responsibilities of the home-front fighter.

Although Pearl Harbor was a shock, America's entry into the war was not exactly unexpected. Americans had hoped we would not have to be a part of the war that was already engulfing Europe and Asia, but most knew there wasn't much chance of escape. On the Monday morning after Pearl Harbor, American homemakers who remembered the food shortages that occurred during World War I, got up early, rushed to the markets, and scooped the sugar from the shelves. The shopping rampage sent prices up and served as a warning to Washington that controls of some sort would be necessary to prevent inflation. Voluntary rationing had not worked during World War I and as early as the summer of 1941 shortages of sugar and coffee had caused grocers to make their own rationing rules—and in some cases print their own rationing coupons—for these items. After Pearl Harbor there were immediate rumors of rationing, and a survey showed that a majority of Americans preferred rationing to taking the chance that things would not be available to everyone. In January of 1942, the Office of Price Administration put into place a system of volunteer local boards to oversee the program. Eventually, ten rationing programs were introduced. Food rationing began on May 5, 1942, with the twenty-eight-stamp "Sugar Book" and went on to include coffee, butter and other fats, canned and frozen goods, and red meat.

Suddenly the job of running a home became much more difficult. Not only were essential food products unavailable but equipment could not be replaced and when local stores did not have the products you needed, there was no gasoline to drive from store to store to hunt for them. Recipes had to be modified because a variety of things from Hawaiian pineapple to Far Eastern spices were gone. Within the next few years home-makers would have to learn the intricacies of Certificate Rationing (for equipment and metal goods), Differential Coupon Rationing (for items such as gasoline and oil that some people needed more than others), Uniform Coupon Rationing (for commodities like sugar and coffee that did not vary greatly within the category), and Point Rationing (for items such as protein sources, fats, and canned goods that did vary—e.g., more desirable cuts of meat "cost" more points).

Hoarding caused coffee, the second food product to be rationed, to come into the program far earlier than would have been necessary based on the wartime conversion of the ships that had been importing the beans. Clearly the nation's caffeine addicts weren't taking any chances on being left without their favorite brew. On November 29, 1942, a quota was set at one pound of coffee every five weeks for every person over fifteen years of age. Fortunately, coffee drinkers could increase the amount of milk they added to each cup because fluid milk was never rationed. (Canned milk, which was still being used in many households because of the lack of refrigeration, was rationed not because of milk scarcity but because of the metal in the cans.)

Homemakers were not alone in the struggle to put the expected daily meals on the table. By early summer of 1942 most of the women's magazines had jumped into the fray with Victory Menus (see page 6), "sugarless" recipes, advice on nutrition, substitutions, quick meals, and warnings about waste, hoarding, and buying on the black market. A notable holdout was *Gourmet* magazine, which made a point of never offering wartime recipes. In answer to a reader's letter that said, "We presume that you are naturally thinking of current food problems and hope that you will rush to print with a series of good *Gourmet* 'ration recipes,'" the March 1943 issue of the fledgling magazine includes the following:

"We are indeed thinking of current food problems, and if you'll look back through our recent issues you'll find that we have been stressing unrationed foods. But why ask for 'ration recipes'—and destroy forthwith in your mind the taste of what are still very savory dishes? The recipes that we give are not for rations; they are for good food, made of the very many ingredients that are still plentiful."

However, in the "Specialties de la Maison" column of the same issue, Iles Brody reviews the restaurant Crillon and notes that "you can enjoy the War Economy Dinner" in the upstairs dining room for just $1.00 while the regular menu costs $1.75 and up. He goes on to list two of the war economy menus: fried smelts, sauce tartare, croquette potatoes, and creamed chicory or veal curry with chutney, rice, and lima beans.

On the other hand, *American Cookery*, once the magazine of the Boston Cooking School, devoted whole issues to dealing with the food problems of the home front. In one issue they went to Chinatown to learn the secret of sprouting soybeans and sent veteran food writer Ida Bailey Allen to a series of military bases to interview the chefs who fed thousands of servicemen each day. She learned all about the proper care of food to prevent waste, new ways to cook leftovers, how proper cooking conserves the nutrients in food, how to make some money-saving soups, and vegetable spreads to take the place of butter. Her article, "What the Army Can Teach You," concluded that "the millions of young men in the United States Army are not only theoretically the best fed in the world, but their physical stamina, proud bearing and high morale are living proof of the efficiency of a well-planned diet made up of appetizing meals of good food prepared to retain full food values. . . . Many of these men are eating balanced meals for the first time in their lives."

Tucked in among all the helpful hints provided by the magazines' home economists are government messages sponsored by the magazines or by advertisers who had converted to war production and had nothing to sell but wanted to keep their names before the public until the war was over. The War Advertising Council produced pages such as the 1943 anti-inflation message which warned, "If You're Making More Money . . . Watch Out! Keep Prices Down" and included the often repeated mantra: "Use it up. Wear it out. Make it do. Or do without." Others featured the "Government's Food Rules" or War Food Administration programs urging homemakers to buy products that were in surplus, such as eggs in the spring of 1944.

Many of the recipes in this chapter come from Victory Dinner menus that appeared in booklets published by the government or the food industry. Each meal was planned to be quick and easy to prepare, provide a balance of nutrients, and use foods that were still available. The remaining recipes each in some way demonstrate a creative response to the problems encountered in the home-front kitchen.

VICTORY DINNER I

Cream of Onion Soup
Tunafish Loaf — Horseradish Sauce
Buttered Peas — Star Salad
Hot Biscuits and Butter
Plum Tarts with Vanilla Ice Cream
Milk   Coffee
Victory Meal Planner, New York State Bureau of Milk Publicity, 1942

VICTORY DINNER II

Swedish Meatballs
Riced Potatoes — Glazed Carrots
Watercress and Grapefruit Salad
Bread — Butter
Butterscotch Pie
Beverage
Victory Meat Extenders, National Live Stock and Meat Board, 1942

VICTORY DINNER III

Meat Patties
Parslied Potatoes
Buttered Beets with Beet Greens
Whole Wheat Bread and Butter
Cottage Pudding with Toffee Sauce
Coffee and Milk
Eating for Fitness, Servel, Inc., 1943

CREAM OF ONION SOUP

★ ★

This is a quick and easy addition to the dinner menu that is a good way to increase the amount of milk in the family's diet with little notice. Although fresh milk prices were sometimes high, it was usually available and not included in the rationing programs that regulated most other protein sources.

4 slices bacon, cut into 1-inch pieces	4 cups milk
3 cups chopped onions	¼ to ½ teaspoon salt
2 tablespoons all-purpose flour	¼ teaspoon ground black pepper

Sauté bacon in a heavy 3-quart saucepan until crisp; remove bacon pieces to a small bowl. Add onions to bacon fat in saucepan and cook, stirring frequently until onions begin to brown.

Stir flour into onions until they are uniformly coated. Gradually add milk, ¼ teaspoon salt, and pepper. Bring to a boil, stirring constantly until thickened. Taste and add more salt, if necessary.

To serve, divide into 4 soup plates or bowls and top with reserved bacon pieces.

4 Servings

"Good News for women who take pride in flavorsome cooking! There will be no shortage of important spices even if imports from Europe and Asia should be completely shut off. Supplies now in this country will last two or three years; after that the United States, Mexico, and South America could grow almost any herb or spice we might need."—*Woman's Home Companion*, May 1942

LADIES' AID SALAD

★ ★

This big-batch salad was good to serve at meetings and working parties for wartime public service groups. These days it can still be found at potlucks and family reunions.

2 quarts water	2 cups diced cooked ham
1 pound macaroni	1 cup chopped celery
1 teaspoon salt	¼ cup chopped pimiento
¼ cup cider vinegar	¼ cup chopped green onion
⅓ cup mayonnaise	3 cups packed salad greens (rinsed,
2 tablespoons light corn syrup	crisped, and broken into pieces)
¼ teaspoon ground black pepper	2 tomatoes, each cut into 6 wedges

Bring water to a boil in a large saucepan. Add macaroni and salt. Cook until macaroni is just tender, about 12 minutes. Drain very well, reserving ½ cup cooking liquid. Immediately combine macaroni and vinegar in a large bowl; set aside 15 minutes.

Meanwhile, stir together mayonnaise, corn syrup, and black pepper. Gradually stir in reserved cooking liquid. Add to macaroni mixture along with ham, celery, pimiento, and onion. Cover and refrigerate until well chilled.

To serve, arrange greens on a very large platter or in a 3-quart bowl. Spoon macaroni mixture into center and garnish with tomato wedges.

12 Servings

> "Often when a housewife would go to market for meat all that seemed available would be bologna or frankfurters at least in the neighborhood stores where many of us shopped in those days."—*Edith Clark, Lake Ann, Michigan*

STAR SALAD

★ ★

Tomato gelatin salads were very popular during the war years. They are easy to make, and tomatoes or tomato juice was pretty consistently available.

1 envelope unflavored gelatin

1½ cups tomato juice

1 tablespoon light corn syrup

1 teaspoon cider vinegar

½ teaspoon Worcestershire sauce

¼ teaspoon celery salt

3 cups salad greens (rinsed, crisped, and broken into pieces)

1 cup cottage cheese

Mayonnaise, optional

Sprinkle gelatin over ½ cup tomato juice in a small saucepan. Set aside 5 minutes to soften.

Meanwhile, combine remaining 1 cup tomato juice, the corn syrup, vinegar, Worcestershire sauce, and celery salt in a medium bowl.

Gently heat the gelatin mixture, stirring constantly until gelatin is dissolved. Add to the juice mixture in the bowl and stir to combine. Divide the mixture between 2 8-ounce drinking glasses; cover and refrigerate until firm—4 to 6 hours.

To serve, divide greens among 6 salad plates. Divide cottage cheese among plates onto center of greens. Quickly dip glasses into a bowl of warm water, loosen gelatin with knife, and unmold onto a rimmed plate. Cut each mold crosswise into 5 slices. Cut each slice into 3 wedges. Arrange 5 wedges around cottage cheese on each salad to resemble a star. Serve with mayonnaise, if desired.

6 Servings

WATERCRESS AND GRAPEFRUIT SALAD

★ ★

This refreshing salad is a nutritionist's dream, which made it popular among wartime homemakers. Citrus fruits were promoted for their high vitamin C content. Here even the dressing provides vitamins.

3 cups watercress (rinsed, crisped, and broken into pieces)

2 large grapefruit (1 pink and 1 white is nice), sectioned

½ cup grapefruit juice (collected while sectioning grapefruit if possible)

2 tablespoons honey

2 tablespoons salad oil

¼ teaspoon salt

⅛ teaspoon hot red pepper (cayenne)

Divide watercress onto 6 chilled salad plates. Put grapefruit sections on top, dividing them onto plates.

Combine grapefruit juice, honey, oil, salt, and pepper in a half-pint jar with a tight lid. Cover and shake until honey has dissolved. Divide onto salads on top of grapefruit sections.

6 Servings

"My mom owned a department store on Beale Street. She worked in the store from 9 till 9 six days a week. I started learning to cook when I was eight years old. Mom bought the 'Bacon' and out of hunger I learned to cook, by way of the telephone. If there was a 'line' at a grocery store I got in the line. I bought whatever goodie was available if we had enough stamps. We would trade it for something we wanted or needed badly."—*Peggy Eaves, Memphis, Tennessee*

WARTIME SPECIAL

Prune Hasty

1½ cups cooked prunes,
   pitted and chopped
¾ cup evaporated milk
¾ cup bread crumbs
½ cup packed light brown
   sugar

½ cup finely chopped nuts
2 teaspoons baking powder
¼ teaspoon salt
1 teaspoon vanilla extract

Preheat oven to 325°F. Generously grease a 1½-quart casserole or pudding mold.

Combine all ingredients and pour into greased casserole. Bake 1 hour or until center is firm. Remove to wire rack and cool 10 minutes. Unmold, if desired, or serve from casserole. Serve hot.

6 Servings

WHITE HOUSE SALAD

★ ★

This is a traditional salad for ladies' luncheons. Some recipes for this mold call for a package of lemon gelatin mix, but the resulting salad is a bit too sweet for today's tastes.

1 package unflavored gelatin	¼ teaspoon salt
1¼ cups water	¼ teaspoon celery salt
⅓ cup lemon juice	½ cup cooked diced carrots
¼ cup light corn syrup	½ cup cooked green peas
2 tablespoons cider vinegar	½ cup chopped celery
½ teaspoon paprika	3 tablespoons mayonnaise

Sprinkle gelatin over ¼ cup water in a small saucepan. Set aside 5 minutes to soften.

Meanwhile, combine remaining 1 cup water, the lemon juice, corn syrup, vinegar, paprika, salt, and celery salt in a medium bowl.

Gently heat gelatin mixture, stirring constantly until gelatin is dissolved. Add to lemon juice mixture and stir to combine. Pour about one third of mixture into a 4-cup ring mold; cover and refrigerate until set—30 to 45 minutes. Cover the bowl of remaining gelatin mixture and set aside at room temperature.

When gelatin layer is set, arrange rows of carrots, peas, and celery equally spaced in the ring mold. Carefully spoon about another third of the gelatin mixture over the vegetables; cover and refrigerate 15 minutes to set surface.

Meanwhile, gradually beat the remaining gelatin mixture into the mayonnaise. Gently spoon the mixture over the vegetable layer. Cover and refrigerate until firm—6 to 8 hours.

To unmold, quickly dip the ring mold into a pan of warm water. Cover the mold with a serving plate and invert. Return to refrigerator 10 minutes to reset the surface before serving.

6 Servings

MONDAY MEAT LOAF

★ ★

In this recipe, the leftovers from Sunday's roast become a nutritious and thrifty meat loaf for Monday's dinner. The word "Monday" in a recipe title often signaled the use of chopped or ground leftover cooked meat in casseroles, meat cakes, or savory loaves. Depending on the type of meat and the flavorings that were used in Sunday's meal, this could taste different every time you made it.

1½ cups day-old white bread crumbs
   (from 4 to 5 slices bread)

½ cup evaporated milk

2 large eggs, lightly beaten

½ cup finely chopped onion

½ cup finely chopped red or green
   bell pepper

¼ cup grated fresh horseradish

½ teaspoon salt

¼ teaspoon ground black pepper

3 cups very finely chopped cooked
   roast beef, pork, or veal (or a
   mixture)

Heat oven to 350°F. Generously grease an 8-inch loaf pan.

Combine bread, milk, eggs, onion, bell pepper, horseradish, salt, and pepper in a medium bowl. Fold in cooked meat.

Spoon meat mixture into greased loaf pan and bake 50 to 60 minutes, until center feels firm when gently pressed. Cool in pan 5 minutes. Remove to platter; slice crosswise into 8 pieces and serve.

8 Servings

PORK SHOULDER ROAST WITH STUFFED ONIONS

★ ★

A March 1944 advertisement says, "Do you know how to turn a pork shoulder into a delicious, succulent roast? Here Armour shows you how—and it's a good trick to know these days when, even though other meats are scarce, your meat man usually has pork." What you could get with ration points was greatly affected by availability, and America's pork producers were able to keep supplies at a high level throughout the war.

1 (5-pound) bone-in pork shoulder roast	8 large (about 3 pounds) onions
¾ teaspoon salt	⅓ cup grated Cheddar cheese
¼ teaspoon ground black pepper	⅓ cup dry bread crumbs
	2 teaspoons butter, melted

Preheat oven to 350°F.

Place pork on a rack in a roasting pan. Sprinkle with ½ teaspoon salt and the pepper. Roast, uncovered, 2½ to 3 hours, or until a meat thermometer inserted in center registers 175°F (see Note).

About 1 hour before pork is done, grease a rimmed baking pan. Bring whole onions and water to cover to a boil in a large saucepan. Cook, covered, until just tender—15 to 20 minutes. Drain well. Remove centers of onions to a chopping board; coarsely chop and mix with cheese.

Place onion shells in a lightly greased, rimmed baking pan; sprinkle inside and out with remaining ¼ teaspoon salt. Divide cheese mixture among onion shells. Combine bread crumbs and butter and divide onto onions. Bake onions 20 minutes or until the cheese melts.

To serve, transfer pork to serving platter and slice crosswise. Add onions to platter. Skim off any fat from broth in roasting pan. Pour broth into small pitcher and serve with pork and onions.

8 Servings

NOTE: In the forties, this roast would have been cooked to 185°F. However, these days the National Pork Producers Council recommends cooking the new lowfat pork to 160°F. I find 170°F to 175°F to be a good compromise for those of us who haven't yet gotten used to pink pork.

"WINS" Rules

Home-front warriors were encouraged to join "Women in National Service." Promoted by the wives of many of the nation's governors, the group created plans that would help homemakers deal with rationing and scarcity in a fair and patriotic way. Their list of food rules were:

Ten Rules for Wartime Eating

1. Keep a list of the seven basic food groups in your kitchen and your purse. Follow it when you plan and when you buy. Substitute within groups.

2. Don't plan to serve meat, fish, poultry, eggs and cheese all the same day.

3. Start the day off right with a breakfast that counts as a real meal. Make cereal with milk the "main dish."

4. Make a hearty soup, or cereal with fruit and milk, your main dish at lunch or supper at least twice a week.

5. Don't waste. Try foods new to you. Eat fresh foods first. Conserve canned supplies. Use bread crumbs in stuffing, bones in soups, remnants of meat or vegetables in stews. Cook potatoes in skins.

6. Help your grocer cut down waste. Don't pinch fruits. Don't toss over vegetables.

7. Start a clean-plate club in your home. Serve smaller portions. Eat it all.

8. Save fats by serving fewer fried foods and rich pastries.

9. Spread the load. Include different protein foods in weekly meal plans.

10. Don't buy food with ration stamps just for the sake of using up the stamps. Don't trade stamps with your neighbor.

SAUSAGE LINK LOAF

This whimsical loaf is reminiscent of the crown roasts of lamb and pork that were almost impossible to get during the war. The flavor here depends on the type of sausage used.

½ (8-ounce) package macaroni
Salt
2 tablespoons vegetable shortening or
  butter (or a mixture)
2 tablespoons flour

1 cup milk
1 cup grated Cheddar cheese
24 (1¾ to 2 pounds) thin 3-inch
  sausage links

Preheat oven to 350°F. Generously grease a 9-inch glass loaf dish.

Cook macaroni in boiling salted water according to package directions. Drain very well.

Meanwhile, in a heavy saucepan, over low heat, melt shortening. Stir in flour and ¼ teaspoon salt until smooth. Very gradually stir in milk; cook over low heat, stirring constantly, until sauce has thickened. Fold in cheese and macaroni.

Arrange sausages around edges of greased loaf dish. Fill center with macaroni mixture.

Place on rimmed baking sheet and bake 60 to 65 minutes or until browned and center feels firm.

To serve, cut loaf crosswise into 8 slices and serve from baking dish.

8 Servings

SWEDISH MEATBALLS

★ ★

A tasty way of extending ground beef, this main dish went on to star as party food in the 1950s and 1960s.

1 pound ground beef	¼ teaspoon ground allspice
1 cup day-old white bread crumbs	¼ teaspoon ground black pepper
(from about 3 slices bread)	1 tablespoon vegetable shortening
1 large egg, lightly beaten	1¼ cups milk
¼ cup finely chopped onion	2 tablespoons all-purpose flour
½ teaspoon salt	

Preheat oven to 350°F.

Combine ground beef, bread, egg, onion, ¼ teaspoon salt, allspice, and pepper. Shape mixture into 24 meatballs.

Heat shortening in a 3-quart Dutch oven. Add meatballs and sauté until brown on all sides; remove to a bowl. Add 1 cup milk to the Dutch oven and bring to a boil. Stir remaining ¼ cup milk into the flour and add to the boiling milk mixture along with remaining ¼ teaspoon salt. Cook, stirring constantly, until thickened. Return meatballs to sauce. Cover and bake 30 minutes. Serve from Dutch oven.

6 Servings

> "Buy-For-A-Week and help your country: Think of the tires and gas you'll save if you lump as many of your weekly food purchases as you can into one order!"—*Del Monte Buy-For-A-Week advertising campaign, 1943*

WARTIME SPECIAL

Whipped Evap

1 teaspoon unflavored gelatin
1 tablespoon cold water
1 cup evaporated milk

1 teaspoon vanilla extract
2 tablespoons confectioners'
   sugar

Combine gelatin and cold water in a cup; set aside 5 minutes for gelatin to soften. Heat ¼ cup evaporated milk in a small saucepan until bubbles form at edge of pan. Stir hot milk into softened gelatin mixture until gelatin is dissolved.

Stir gelatin mixture into remaining milk in a small bowl. Stir in vanilla; cover and refrigerate until very cold.

Beat evaporated milk mixture with a rotary or electric beater until light and fluffy, gradually adding the confectioners' sugar as you beat. Cover and store in the refrigerator.

3 Cups

(NOTE: This was used in place of heavy cream when it was not available.)

SQUASH BISCUITS

★ ★

A half cup of leftover whipped winter squash lends sweetness and a golden color to these busy-day biscuits. In our war against waste every little bit counted. "Drop" biscuits save time by eliminating the extra step of rolling and cutting the biscuit dough.

2 cups unsifted all-purpose flour	⅓ cup shortening
3 tablespoons light brown sugar	½ cup milk
3 teaspoons baking powder	½ cup winter squash puree (see
¼ teaspoon salt	Note)

Preheat oven to 375°F. Lightly grease a baking sheet.

Combine flour, brown sugar, baking powder, and salt in a medium bowl. Cut in shortening with a pastry blender or 2 knives until the mixture forms coarse crumbs.

Combine milk and squash puree. Add to flour mixture and stir together just until all flour mixture has been moistened. Spoon out onto greased baking sheet to make 12 biscuits. Bake for 15 to 20 minutes or until lightly browned. Cool 5 minutes on baking sheet. Remove to serving basket and serve warm.

12 Biscuits

NOTE: Whip cubes of cooked winter squash or use frozen whipped winter squash if you don't have leftovers.

> "Ever try cooking with a Percolator? . . . With no other equipment than a large electric percolator you can turn out a variety of satisfying stews, soups and chowders. You can't broil or fry in a percolator—but its stored heat is ideal for cooking meats and vegetables slowly."—*McCall's*, September 1944

WHOLE-WHEAT BREAD

★ ★

Baking homemade bread was doubly rewarding at a time when everyone was concerned about nutrition as well as the physical and psychological factors related to mothers working away from home.

1 cup milk

¼ cup maple syrup

3 tablespoons vegetable shortening or
   butter (or a mixture)

¾ teaspoon salt

¼ cup warm (105° to 110°F) water

1 package active dry yeast

3 to 3½ cups unsifted all-purpose
   flour

1 cup unsifted whole-wheat flour

1 large egg, lightly beaten

Heat milk in a small saucepan over medium heat until bubbles form at edge of pan; stir in maple syrup, shortening, and salt. Transfer to a large bowl and set aside to cool to 105° to 110°F.

Combine warm water and yeast in a cup and set aside for yeast to soften.

When milk mixture has cooled, add 3 cups all-purpose flour, the whole wheat flour, beaten egg, and yeast mixture; stir until a soft dough forms. Turn dough out onto a work surface sprinkled with some of remaining ½ cup flour. Knead 5 minutes, adding as much of remaining flour as necessary to make the dough manageable. Place dough in a greased bowl, cover, and set aside in a warm place until double in size—about 1 hour.

Grease a 9-inch loaf pan. Shape dough into a log and fit into greased pan. Set aside in a warm place until double in size—about 45 minutes.

Preheat oven to 350°F. Bake 40 to 45 minutes, or until golden brown and loaf sounds hollow when tapped on top. Cool at least 30 minutes before cutting.

12 Servings

BUTTERSCOTCH PIE

★ ★

I rediscovered my double boiler while testing the recipes in this book. Many wartime recipes use a double boiler to take the watching out of making sauces and sweet desserts. It certainly makes it easy to prepare this old-fashioned dessert without scorching it.

3 cups milk	1 teaspoon vanilla extract
⅓ cup cornstarch	1 (9-inch) baked pastry shell
¾ cup packed light brown sugar	½ cup heavy cream
1 tablespoon butter	2 teaspoons confectioners' sugar
¼ teaspoon salt	

Bring 2½ cups milk to boiling in top of a double boiler over boiling water. Combine cornstarch and remaining ½ cup milk in a cup; add gradually to milk in double boiler and cook, stirring occasionally until thickened.

Add brown sugar, butter, and salt to milk mixture. Return to boiling and cook 3 minutes. Remove from heat; stir in vanilla and pour into pastry shell. Cool to room temperature. Cover loosely and refrigerate until firm—3 to 4 hours—before cutting.

Just before serving, beat cream with confectioners' sugar. Spoon a dollop on each serving of pie.

6 Servings

"Because of rationing I had a new way of life. I made lye soap to wash baby clothes, picked wild greens, canned all garden vegetables and fruit, helped raise broilers and milk 29 cows by hand. We butchered our own meat, also caught fish and had frog legs."—*Marjorie Marzolf, Salina, Kansas*

COTTAGE PUDDING WITH TOFFEE SAUCE

★ ★

Cottage Pudding is a thrifty way of making a delicious, warm dessert out of pieces of day-old cake that might otherwise go to waste. (Also see Salvage Pudding, page 24, which uses day-old cake crumbs.) There are many toppings that can be used; lemon, cherry, and chocolate are other popular ones.

4 (3-inch) squares or wedges day-old, unfrosted, vanilla, spice, or pound cake

⅓ cup evaporated milk, undiluted

⅓ cup light corn syrup

⅓ cup dark corn syrup

1 teaspoon butter

1 teaspoon vanilla extract

Preheat oven to 350°F. Arrange cake on a wire rack that fits on top of a 9-inch square baking pan. Place the pan in the oven; fill with boiling water to within 1 inch of the top of the pan. Place rack full of cake on top of pan. Cover with oiled aluminum foil or an inverted bowl. Heat cake until sauce is prepared—no longer than 10 minutes.

Combine evaporated milk, light and dark corn syrups, and butter. Bring to a boil over medium heat, stirring constantly. Remove from heat and stir in vanilla.

To serve, place cake on individual dessert plates; divide sauce over cake pieces and serve immediately.

4 Servings

"We Americans love slogans. The nutritionists shout: 'Food Will Win the War.' If a war lasts more than a year or two, that nation which is best fed, both in the field and at home is bound to win!"—*Redbook*, February 1942

PLUM TARTS

★ ★

Canned plums make a quick filling for these little tarts. The tart shells can be baked several days ahead and kept in an airtight tin.

1 recipe Flaky Pastry (page 211)	2 tablespoons cornstarch
2 (15-ounce) cans purple plums in heavy syrup	¼ teaspoon vanilla extract
	⅛ teaspoon salt

Preheat oven to 400°F. Divide Flaky Pastry into 6 balls. Roll out each to a 5-inch round; fit each into a 3-inch tart pan and trim edge ¼ inch above top of pan. Pierce bottom of pastry with the tines of a fork and bake until golden and crisp—8 to 10 minutes.

Meanwhile, thoroughly drain plums, reserving the syrup. Combine 1¼ cups of the syrup, the cornstarch, vanilla, and salt. Bring to a boil over medium heat, stirring constantly until thickened. Pour into a small bowl and set aside.

Quarter plums and remove seeds. Stir into sauce and divide into tart shells. Cool to room temperature before serving.

6 Servings

The introductory page of the 1943 General Foods Corporation booklet *Recipes for Today* is a letter to Uncle Sam signed, "Your loving niece, Victorianna." She clearly defines the concept of the home-front warrior when she says, "I am not a WAVE nor a WAAC, but I am working for you just the same, all in the big cause of supplying more food for our soldiers and our armies of civilians and allies. And you'll be glad to know I have advanced myself from rookie, 3rd class to kitchen lieutenant since Pearl Harbor." The page goes on to list Victorianna's Wartime Food Rules:

1. Get down to good, plain food.
2. Work harder planning, buying, and cooking.
3. Buy the most for the money.
4. Learn all about the food rations.
5. Never waste a bit of food.

SALVAGE PUDDING

Professional bakers have always had a repertoire of recipes made from the crumbs of unsold cakes and cookies. During the war, that idea moved into the home-front kitchen. Recipes such as this one, which uses cake and cookie crumbs, became invaluable in the fight against waste and in the effort to provide sweet desserts without exhausting the family's supply of rationed sugar.

2 cups crumbs of vanilla or spice
    cookies or cake
1 cup milk
1 cup unsifted all-purpose flour
½ cup light corn syrup
1 large egg, beaten
¼ cup vegetable shortening or butter
    (or a mixture), melted

1 teaspoon baking powder
½ teaspoon ground cinnamon
¼ teaspoon ground cloves
¼ teaspoon ground nutmeg
¼ teaspoon salt
½ cup dark seedless raisins
Vanilla ice cream, optional

Preheat oven to 350°F (see Note). Grease a 6-cup ring mold. Combine crumbs and milk in a medium bowl. Set aside 10 minutes for crumbs to absorb milk.

Add flour, corn syrup, egg, shortening, baking powder, cinnamon, cloves, nutmeg, and salt to crumb mixture. Stir just until combined. Fold in raisins. Transfer to greased ring mold. Cover with greased aluminum foil.

Bake 35 to 40 minutes or until center springs back when gently pressed. Remove foil and cool in pan 5 minutes. Invert onto serving plate and serve hot with vanilla ice cream, if desired.

8 Servings

NOTE: This recipe could be steamed in a covered 1½-quart pudding mold for 2 to 2½ hours, if desired.

2

EAT TO WIN

★★★★★★★★★★★★★★★★★★★★

Peanut Butter Date Bread

Cheese Custards with Chives

Peanut Butter Popcorn Balls

Corned Beef Puffs

Peanut Gems

Limas Fort McArthur

Soybean Chili

Creamed Dried Beef on Baked Potatoes

Soy Rocks

Cereal Rolls

Meat Loaf with Soy

Mock Sausage Patties

Meat Pie with Soy Biscuit Crust

Ham Loaf with Molasses

Cornmeal Chicken Livers

Molasses Rye Bread

Liver Loaf

Uncle Sam's Food Rules

Rule 1: Milk and Milk Products—at least a pint of milk for everyone, more for children, or use cheese, evaporated or dried milk in cooked dishes.

Rule 2: Oranges, Tomatoes and Grapefruit—at least one of these or substitute raw cabbage or salad greens.

Rule 3: Green or Yellow Vegetables—at least a big helping or more, some fresh, some canned, or quick frozen.

Rule 4: Other Vegetables, Fruits—potatoes, other vegetables, or fruits in season, fresh, dried, canned, or quick-frozen.

Rule 5: Bread and Cereals—whole grain products or enriched cereals, white bread, and flour.

Rule 6: Meat, Poultry, or Fish—as available, substitute dried beans, peas, or nuts occasionally.

Rule 7: Eggs—at least 3 or 4 a week, cooked as you choose or in recipes.

Rule 8: Butter and Other Spreads—including "vitaminized" margarine, vitamin-rich fats, peanut butter, and similar spreads.

Then eat other foods you also like.

Moms have always been concerned about good nutrition; it's part of their job. But the years of the Great Depression made it very difficult for many families to get the healthy foods they needed. As America's entry into World War II became imminent, newspapers editorialized about the poorly nourished men who did not qualify for the armed services and about the high percentage of the population that was underfed, thereby affecting the nation's defense efforts. Government food economists estimated that "one-third of America's families are below the safety line of nutrition." Slogans such as "Eat the Right Food, U.S. Needs US Strong," "Nutrition Lessons Mean Nothing Unless You Take Them to the Table," "First Aid to Nutrition—Your Refrigerator," "Quick-frozen Foods for Quick, Nutritious Meals," and "Vitamins Vital for Victory" reflected these concerns. They had a ready audience in America's homemakers. A healthy nation was crucial to winning the war and the kitchen was declared the first line of defense. New developments in the field of nutrition made it a "hot" topic and articles containing recipes high in vitamins and protein were the rage.

As the nation's needs and wartime programs changed, the government's food-related guidelines changed. By close interaction with magazine editors and through joint publicity programs with the Advertising Council, the government's concerns quickly appeared in both editorial and advertising pages. In 1942, the eight-category daily food plan entitled "Our Government Recommends—Every Day, Eat This Way" and often called "Uncle Sam's Food Rules" defined the national nutrition program of the Office of Defense Health and Welfare Services (opposite page). It appeared in both editorial and advertising pages promoting home-front health through better nutrition. By 1943, the system was pared down to 7 categories. The pamphlet, "Eating for Fitness," explained, "Your Government with the help of food experts and nutritionists has prepared a simple, easy-to-understand chart of foods to eat for fitness. This chart condenses all the essential requirements of good nutrition into a simple set of food rules, the "Daily Seven" (see Box on page 28). The new system was at first presented in the same format as the old one, but soon the easier to read "Basic Seven" wheel appeared everywhere promoting "The Right Food—Plenty of It."

After years of worrying about having enough to eat, there was no thought of cutting back just yet. The government clearly noted that you could have anything you wanted in addition to the foods listed in its recommendations. In looking at recipe portion sizes, it's worth noting that servings of 6 or even 8 ounces of meat per person were not unusual and that when a recipe called for the 4 ounces per serving we consider average today, it was called a "meat-stretcher." A variety of ingredients were added to recipes to increase the protein they supplied. Cooked soybeans and soy flour played a prominent part in adding enrichment to recipes as did evaporated milk. Whole articles were devoted to suggestions for sneaking nutrients into daily meals in order to trick husbands and children into eating properly. This chapter contains those recipes with added "high nutrient" ingredients. Peanut butter is the high-protein addition to Peanut Butter Date Bread, Peanut Butter Popcorn Balls, and Peanut Gems. "Soya" products lend enrichment to Soybean Chili, Soy Rocks, Meatloaf with Soy, and Meat Pie with Soy Biscuit Crust. Condensed milk is the secret ingredient in Cheese Custards with Chives and Corned Beef Puffs. Whole-grain and liver dishes, always high on Mothers' good-for-you list, are here too.

The Daily Seven

Group One: Green and Yellow Vegetables

Group Two: Oranges, Tomatoes, Grapefruit

Group Three: Potatoes and Other Vegetables and Fruits

Group Four: Milk and Milk Products

Group Five: Meat, Poultry, Fish, or Eggs

Group Six: Bread, Flour, and Cereals

Group Seven: Butter and Fortified Margarine

In addition to the basic seven . . . eat any other food you want.

PEANUT BUTTER DATE BREAD

Peanut butter was frequently used as a substitute for rationed fats in breads, muffins, biscuits, and other baked goods. This recipe calls for cutting the peanut butter into the flour mixture just as you would shortening.

2 cups unsifted all-purpose flour
½ cup packed light brown sugar
4 teaspoons baking powder
¼ teaspoon salt
¾ cup smooth peanut butter
½ cup chopped dates

2 large eggs
½ cup evaporated milk plus ½ cup water or 1 cup milk
2 tablespoons chopped peanuts, optional

Preheat oven to 350°F. Grease a 9-inch loaf pan.

Combine flour, brown sugar, baking powder, and salt in a large bowl. Cut in peanut butter with a pastry blender or 2 knives to make coarse crumbs. Stir in dates.

Beat egg in a small bowl. Gradually beat in milk and water. Add to dry ingredients and stir just until dry ingredients are moistened. Don't overbeat. Transfer batter to greased loaf pan. Sprinkle with chopped peanuts, if desired.

Bake 55 to 60 minutes or until a toothpick inserted in the center comes out clean. Cool to room temperature and serve or pack in an airtight container.

12 Servings

PEANUT BUTTER POPCORN BALLS

★ ★

Peanut butter adds flavor as well as protein to these holiday sweets. They can be wrapped in wax paper and then in colored tissue paper to make a colorful centerpiece or gift.

1 cup light molasses	½ cup peanut butter
⅔ cup light corn syrup	½ teaspoon vanilla extract
1 tablespoon vinegar	3 quarts popped corn
1 teaspoon salt	

Combine molasses, corn syrup, vinegar, and salt in a heavy 3-quart saucepan. Bring to a boil over medium heat, stirring frequently until mixture reaches 250°F or until a little syrup dropped into cold water forms a hard ball. Remove from heat and stir in peanut butter and vanilla.

While syrup is cooking, spread out popcorn in a deep roasting pan. When peanut butter mixture has been combined, pour immediately over popcorn and stir until popcorn is evenly coated.

Lightly oil hands and shape mixture into 12 balls. Set aside to cool completely.

12 Servings

> "The WACS are doing a man-size job, but they are not eating the way the men do, reported Lieutenant Edna Cox of the WAC Training Center, Daytona Beach, Florida, at the recent American Dietetics Association Convention in Pittsburg, Pennsylvania. The women eat about half as much bread, fewer potatoes, more salads, and less meat. They eat less sugar at the table, but they like desserts."—*American Cookery*, December 1943

PEANUT GEMS

A 1942 Gold Medal flour advertisement suggests giving children peanut butter cookies and milk as a "Vitamin Snack" when they are hungry. These cookies travel well because the syrup that was added to the recipe to replace part of the sugar makes them less fragile than the usual peanut butter cookies.

1¾ cups unsifted all-purpose flour
1 teaspoon baking powder
½ teaspoon baking soda
¼ teaspoon salt
½ cup brown sugar
½ cup peanut butter

½ cup vegetable shortening or butter
  (or a mixture)
⅔ cup dark corn syrup
1 large egg
½ cup unsalted roasted peanuts,
  finely chopped

Preheat oven to 350°F. Grease 2 baking sheets.

Stir together flour, baking powder, soda, and salt. Beat together brown sugar, peanut butter, and shortening in a medium bowl until fluffy. Beat in corn syrup and egg. Stir in dry ingredients. Drop dough by rounded teaspoonfuls onto greased baking sheets. Sprinkle peanuts on top; pat to flatten slightly. Bake 10 to 12 minutes or until edges begin to brown and centers are set. Cool and serve or pack in an airtight container.

48 Cookies

"We did not have a freezer, but we did have a cold storage business in town where you rented a huge basket, usually 12 to 15 feet up in the air, where we raced on our bicycles to get the food there as soon as possible."—*Sis Baile, Cherry Hill, New Jersey*

SOYBEAN CHILI

★ ★

Cooked dried soybeans were used to extend the protein in recipes that contained just a little meat for flavor. They seemed to disappear from the retail market in the 1950s and 1960s and return as if newly discovered in the 1980s and 1990s.

¾ cup dried soybeans	1 pint home-canned or 1
¼ cup diced salt pork or slab bacon	(15-ounce) can tomatoes
½ pound ground chuck	2 cups water
1 medium onion, chopped (½ cup)	1 tablespoon chili powder
	½ to ¾ teaspoon salt

Day before serving, pick through soybeans, discarding any discolored ones or any foreign material. Rinse soybeans and place in a medium bowl with cold water to cover. Cover and refrigerate 6 to 8 hours. Drain, add water to cover, and cook until tender—1½ to 2 hours, depending upon dryness of soybeans. Drain thoroughly.

To prepare chili, sauté salt pork in large heavy saucepan until browned. Add ground chuck and onion; sauté, stirring occasionally, until well browned.

Stir in drained, cooked soybeans, tomatoes, water, chili powder, and salt to taste. Bring to a boil over high heat; reduce heat to low and simmer, stirring occasionally, 20 minutes. Serve.

4 Servings

> "We have heard of sweet potato candy for quite a while, now other foods are entering the confectionery field. Candy high in vitamins and nutritive values will be made in the future from wheat germ, soy and peanut products, our old friend cottonseed, and corn products."—*American Cookery*, February 1944

SOY ROCKS

★ ★

Spicy and full of good-for-you ingredients, these cookies were an acceptable snack for children. They also travel well, so they were a good choice for lunches and gifts.

1½ cups unsifted all-purpose flour

½ cup soy flour

1½ teaspoons ground cinnamon

½ teaspoon baking powder

½ teaspoon baking soda

½ teaspoon salt

½ teaspoon ground nutmeg

¼ teaspoon ground cloves

1 cup packed light brown sugar

½ cup vegetable shortening or butter (or a mixture)

2 large eggs

¼ cup buttermilk

½ cup chopped nuts

½ cup dark seedless raisins

Preheat oven to 375°F. Grease 2 baking sheets.

Stir together all-purpose flour, soy flour, cinnamon, baking powder, baking soda, salt, nutmeg, and cloves.

Beat together brown sugar and shortening. Beat in eggs, one at a time, until combined.

Stir dry ingredients into shortening mixture along with buttermilk just until combined. Fold in nuts and raisins.

Drop batter by rounded teaspoonfuls onto greased baking sheets and bake 10 to 12 minutes or until a toothpick inserted in the center of one comes out clean. Cool and serve or pack in an airtight container.

36 Cookies

MEAT LOAF WITH SOY

★ ★

A Good Housekeeping *article entitled "Good As Ever Old-Fashioned Dishes Made to Fit Our Times" redeveloped some favorite old recipes to meet wartime needs. Extended with soy flour, a loaf similar to this one provided lots of protein while saving meat points.*

1½ pounds ground chuck	¼ cup ketchup
¾ cup soy flour	2 tablespoons prepared horseradish
⅓ cup tomato juice	1 tablespoon prepared mustard
1 large egg, lightly beaten	1 tablespoon Worcestershire sauce
¼ cup finely chopped onion	1 teaspoon salt
¼ cup finely chopped green bell	¼ teaspoon ground black pepper
pepper	

Heat oven to 350°F. Grease a 9-inch loaf pan.

Combine chuck, soy flour, tomato juice, egg, onion, bell pepper, ketchup, horseradish, mustard, Worcestershire sauce, salt, and pepper in a medium bowl.

Spoon meat mixture into greased loaf pan and bake until center feels firm when gently pressed—about 1 hour. Cool in pan 5 minutes. Remove to platter; slice crosswise into 8 pieces and serve immediately.

8 Servings

WARTIME SPECIAL

Jellied Vegetable Entree

1 package lemon or lime
    flavored gelatin mix

¾ cup hot water

1 bouillon cube

1 cup cold water

3 tablespoons cider vinegar

½ teaspoon salt

1 teaspoon onion juice

⅔ cup cooked diced carrots

⅔ cup cooked peas

⅛ teaspoon cayenne

2 hard-cooked eggs, peeled
    and quartered lengthwise

Dissolve gelatin mix and bouillon cube in boiling water. Stir in cold water, vinegar, salt, and onion juice. Chill until thickened.

Spoon 1-inch gelatin into gelatin mold. Arrange egg wedges around side of mold. Refrigerate until firm—30 minutes. Fold remaining ingredients into remaining gelatin, cover, and set aside at room temperature.

When gelatin in mold is firm, add remaining gelatin mixture. Chill until firm. Unmold and serve.

MEAT PIE WITH SOY BISCUIT CRUST

★ ★

The soy biscuits that add nutrition to this flavorful beef pie can stand alone. Prepare just the biscuits as directed and bake on a cookie sheet to serve with jam for breakfast, lunch, or dinner. Or split them and serve with leftover meat and gravy for a quick lunch.

2 slices bacon, cut into 1-inch pieces

1¼ cups unsifted all-purpose flour

½ teaspoon salt

⅛ teaspoon ground black pepper

1¼ pounds stewing beef, cut into 1-inch cubes

1 onion, coarsely chopped

2 cups water

¼ teaspoon dried thyme leaves

3 tablespoons soy flour

1½ teaspoons baking powder

3 tablespoons vegetable shortening or butter (or a mixture)

⅓ cup milk

4 small red potatoes, scrubbed and quartered

2 carrots, cut into 1-inch-thick pieces

2 stalks celery, cut into 1-inch-thick pieces

1 small green bell pepper, cut into 1-inch pieces

Preheat oven to 375°F. Sauté bacon in a 4-quart Dutch oven just until it begins to brown. Remove to a medium bowl; reserve drippings in Dutch oven.

Meanwhile, in a pie plate or on a piece of wax paper, combine ¼ cup flour, ¼ teaspoon salt, and the pepper. Add beef cubes and turn to coat completely; reserve any leftover flour mixture. Add beef to bacon drippings in Dutch oven and sauté until well browned—about 5 minutes on each side. Remove beef to bowl with bacon.

Add onion to Dutch oven and sauté until browned—about 3 minutes. If any flour was left from coating beef cubes, stir it in here. Return beef and bacon to Dutch oven along with water and thyme; bring to a boil, cover, and bake 1 hour.

About 10 minutes before beef has finished cooking, combine remaining 1 cup all-purpose flour, the soy flour, baking powder, and remaining ¼ teaspoon salt. Cut in shortening with a pastry blender or 2 knives until the mixture forms fine crumbs. Add milk and stir together.

Pat out to ½-inch thickness on a floured board. Cut into rounds with a 3-inch cutter.

When beef has cooked 1 hour, stir in vegetables; place biscuits on top of stew and return to oven to bake for 20 to 25 minutes or until vegetables are tender and biscuits are baked through.

6 Servings

CORNMEAL CHICKEN LIVERS

★ ★

During the war, when I was a child, my grandmother used to take me to a store in Philadelphia where they sold only chickens. In addition to live and dressed chickens, they had a whole case of parts, including livers and gizzards. My grandmother would buy a chicken and have it cut into pieces, then add some extra drumsticks for the children and a cardboard container of livers to make this way. In the 1950s when chicken parts finally came to our small town, my mother would often make just the livers for dinner with parsleyed potatoes and a vegetable and I would get a little wax paper package of the leftovers in my lunch.

1 pound chicken livers	1 to 2 tablespoons bacon fat or
1 large egg	vegetable shortening
⅓ cup yellow cornmeal	¼ teaspoon salt
	¼ teaspoon ground black pepper

Toss livers with egg in a medium bowl. Spread out cornmeal in a pie plate. Scoop livers, a few at a time into the cornmeal. Toss to coat.

Heat 1 tablespoon bacon fat in large skillet. Fry chicken livers until brown on all sides, adding more fat if needed. Remove and drain well; sprinkle with salt and pepper. Keep warm until all have been cooked. Serve immediately.

4 Servings

"My mother and I gardened and canned vegetables and preserved fruit, jam and jellies. I sewed clothes for my daughters out of feed sacks, because material was scarce. We all worked for the war effort by buying war bonds, giving blood to the Red Cross (I gave 8 times) and we walked most places to save gas. Butter, sugar, coffee, tea, meat and canned goods were rationed, so it took a lot of ingenuity to cook delicious and nutritious meals."—*Mary Snyder, Everett, Washington*

LIVER LOAF

★ ★

When you were a child, how often did you hear, "Eat your liver"? Liver is nutritious and was easier to find than the "high point" red meats, so every home-front warrior knew she had to find some way to make it attractive to her family. Recipes like this one were designed to make the job easier. This is also very good for sandwiches the next day.

6 strips bacon	½ cup grated carrots
¼ cup finely chopped onion	1 large egg
¼ cup finely chopped green bell pepper	¼ cup milk
	¼ cup finely chopped pimiento
1 pound liver (beef if you can get it, but pork or lamb are good substitutes)	1 teaspoon Worcestershire sauce
	¼ teaspoon salt
	¼ teaspoon ground black pepper
3 slices firm white bread	White Sauce, optional (recipe follows)

Preheat oven to 350°F. Grease an 8-inch loaf pan.

Finely chop 2 strips bacon. Sauté chopped bacon with onion and green pepper until bacon is crisp and vegetables have started to brown. Drain very well.

Grind liver and bread together with a food grinder (or processor). Combine ground liver mixture with bacon and vegetable mixture, carrots, egg, milk, pimiento, Worcestershire sauce, salt, and black pepper.

Spoon liver loaf mixture into greased loaf pan. Cut remaining strips bacon in half. Arrange diagonally over top of meat mixture. Bake, uncovered, 45 to 50 minutes or until center of the loaf feels firm when gently pressed and meat thermometer inserted in center registers 170°F.

To serve, cut loaf crosswise into ½-inch slices and serve with white sauce, if desired.

WHITE SAUCE: Combine ¼ cup unsifted all-purpose flour, ½ teaspoon salt, and ⅛ teaspoon ground black pepper in a heavy 1-quart saucepan. Gradually stir in 2 cups milk until smooth. Bring to a boil over medium heat, stirring constantly until thickened. Stir in 1 teaspoon butter.

6 Servings

Eat the Right Foods

Based on the U. S. Government's Guide to Good Nutrition

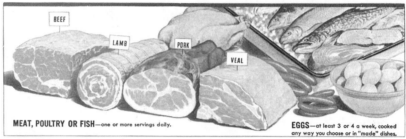

MEAT, POULTRY OR FISH—one or more servings daily.

EGGS—at least 3 or 4 a week, cooked any way you choose or in "made" dishes.

VEGETABLES—Green, Leafy and Yellow— one big helping or more a day—some raw, some cooked or canned.

MILK
—at least a pint a day (more for children)
—or cheese or evaporated or dried milk.

ORANGES, TOMATOES, GRAPEFRUIT —one of these at least once a day.

POTATOES, APPLES, BANANAS — or other vegetables or fruits every day.

BREAD AND CEREAL— enriched bread, enriched flour, whole grain products, macaroni, spaghetti.

FATS, SWEETS and seasonings as you like them

The foods shown here are on the government's model menu for well-balanced meals, which have so much to do with the health, vigor, morale and efficiency of the nation.

In proper proportion and amount, they combine all of the elements of good nutrition—proteins, vitamins, fats, carbohydrates, iron, copper, calcium, phosphorus and other essential minerals.

These foods are needed in summer, just as they are in winter.

In planning balanced meals with meat, as most housewives do, remember that the thriftier cuts contain the same nutrients as the more familiar ones—plus, of course, that good meat flavor. Your meat-man will help you in your selection.

This Seal means that all statements made in this advertisement are acceptable to the Council on Foods and Nutrition of the American Medical Association.

AMERICAN MEAT INSTITUTE... Chicago

June 1942

CHEESE CUSTARDS WITH CHIVES

★ ★

This recipe was suggested as a way to get picky eaters to include some dairy products in their diet. It is flavorful and satisfying and can serve as a protein-rich vegetarian main dish.

1½ cups evaporated milk plus ½ cup
   water
1 cup cubed day-old white bread
3 large eggs, well beaten
1 tablespoon finely chopped chives

½ teaspoon dry mustard
¼ teaspoon salt
⅛ teaspoon hot red pepper (cayenne)
1¼ cups grated Cheddar cheese
Boiling water

Combine milk-water mixture and bread in a medium bowl; set aside 5 minutes.

Preheat oven to 325°F. Generously grease 6 small custard cups or ramekins. Place cups in a shallow roasting pan.

Beat eggs, chives, mustard, salt, and red pepper into milk mixture. Fold in cheese. Divide among greased custard cups.

Place roasting pan with filled cups in oven; fill pan with boiling water to reach 1-inch up sides of custard cups. Bake 1 hour or until a knife inserted in center of one comes out clean.

To serve, loosen custards from edges of cups with a knife and invert onto serving plates.

6 Servings

"The Army and Navy are using enriched flour and bread because of the extra health values they offer at no extra cost. You're in the Army, too! It's your patriotic duty to give your family these health values by using enriched bread and flour."—*Good Housekeeping*, November 1942

WARTIME SPECIAL

Molasses Lemon Pudding

1 cup granulated sugar
½ cup cornstarch
⅓ cup cold water
1 teaspoon salt
2 cups boiling water

½ cup molasses
2 eggs
⅓ cup lemon juice
2 teaspoons grated lemon peel
2 tablespoons butter

Combine sugar, cornstarch, cold water, and salt in the top of a double boiler. Stir in boiling water and molasses. Cook over hot water until thick. Beat eggs until very light. Gradually stir in some of pudding; return mixture to remaining pudding in top of double boiler and cook until very thick. Fold in lemon juice, butter, and lemon peel. Divide into dessert dishes.

CORNED BEEF PUFFS

★ ★

There is a big difference in flavor and moistness between canned and home-cooked corned beef. Use leftover home-cooked if you have a choice. If you don't have any, use canned. The results will be just as good, but different.

1½ cups chopped cooked corned beef	¼ cup finely chopped onion
1 cup chopped cooked potatoes	1 teaspoon prepared mustard
½ cup evaporated milk	¼ teaspoon ground black pepper
1 large egg, separated	

Preheat oven to 400°F. Lightly grease a rimmed baking sheet.

Combine corned beef, potatoes, milk, egg yolk, onion, mustard, and pepper in a large bowl.

Beat egg white in another bowl until stiff peaks form; fold into corned beef mixture. Divide mixture into 6 equal ovals on greased baking sheet. Bake until puffed and firm—15 to 20 minutes. If necessary, place under broiler 1 minute to brown.

6 Servings

"One road to Victory lies across your meal table—you can help make America healthy and strong by selecting and serving the foods that will keep your family healthy and strong."—*Eating for Fitness: Home Volunteers Guide to Better Nutrition, 1943*

LIMAS FORT McARTHUR

★ ★

The mild buttery flavor of lima beans lends itself to a variety of combinations. This savory side dish inspired by an unknown army chef could become a main dish with the addition of just a little more bacon or some leftover ham.

3 cups drained, cooked or canned
  dried lima beans
½ cup finely chopped onion
½ cup finely chopped green bell
  pepper
1 teaspoon packed light brown sugar
1 teaspoon dry mustard

½ teaspoon salt
¼ teaspoon ground black pepper
¼ teaspoon ground mace
¼ teaspoon poultry seasoning
1 cup evaporated milk
3 slices bacon, halved

Preheat oven to 375°F. Grease a 1½- to 2-quart casserole.

Combine limas, onion, bell pepper, brown sugar, mustard, salt, black pepper, mace, and poultry seasoning in greased casserole. Pour milk over mixture and top with bacon.

Bake until the bacon is crisp and the mixture bubbles—30 to 35 minutes. Serve from casserole.

4 Servings

"According to a report from OWI (Office of War Information), hardly one of 800 women questioned in a recent survey sent their husbands off with what nutritionists believe is an adequate breakfast."—*American Cookery*, January 1944

CREAMED DRIED BEEF ON BAKED POTATOES

★ ★

Evaporated milk makes a creamy sauce and adds a little protein to the small amount of meat in this recipe. Despite all the rude jokes about Creamed Dried Beef, it is still pretty comforting, and the substitution of a baked potato makes a heartier meal than when it is served on toast.

4 large baking potatoes

¼ cup margarine

¼ cup chopped onion

¼ cup chopped green bell pepper

¼ cup unsifted all-purpose flour

¼ teaspoon ground black pepper

1½ cups evaporated milk plus ½ cup water

¼ pound dried beef, torn into small pieces

1 teaspoon Worcestershire sauce

Preheat oven to 375°F. Scrub potatoes and pierce each one once with point of a knife. Place on oven rack and bake until tender—50 to 60 minutes.

When potatoes have baked 45 minutes, heat margarine in heavy 2-quart saucepan. Add onion and bell pepper and sauté until golden. Stir in flour and black pepper until vegetables are well coated.

Gradually beat evaporated milk and water into vegetable mixture. Bring to a boil over low heat, stirring constantly until thickened. Fold in dried beef and Worcestershire sauce; cook 2 minutes longer.

To serve, split potatoes and place each on a dinner plate. Divide creamed dried beef mixture onto potatoes and serve.

4 Servings

CEREAL ROLLS

★ ★

Hot cereal was promoted as an ideal way to prepare families for a busy cold-weather day. And if any was left over, it was a head start toward making nutritious rolls for the evening meal.

⅔ cup milk

4 tablespoons vegetable shortening or
   butter (or a mixture)

2 tablespoons light brown sugar

1 teaspoon salt

¼ cup warm (105° to 110°F) water

1 package active dry yeast

½ cup leftover cooked oatmeal or
   granular wheat cereals

3½ to 4½ cups unsifted all-purpose
   flour

Heat milk in a small saucepan over medium heat until bubbles form at edge of pan; stir in shortening, brown sugar, and salt.

Combine warm water and yeast in a cup and set aside for yeast to soften.

Gradually beat hot milk mixture into cereal in a large bowl until thoroughly combined. Set aside to cool to 105° to 110°F.

Add 3½ cups flour and the yeast mixture to cereal mixture and stir until a soft dough forms.

Turn dough out onto a work surface sprinkled with some of remaining 1 cup flour. Knead 5 minutes, adding as much flour as necessary to make the dough manageable. Place dough in a greased bowl, cover, and set aside in a warm place until double in size—about 1 hour.

Grease a 12-cup muffin pan. Divide dough into 12 equal pieces. Shape each piece into a ball and place in greased pan. Set aside in a warm place until double in size—about 45 minutes.

Preheat oven to 400°F. Bake rolls about 25 minutes or until golden brown and roll sounds hollow when tapped on the top. Cool at least 15 minutes before serving.

12 Servings

MOCK SAUSAGE PATTIES

★ ★

This recipe is based on one the Post Cereal company promoted. It can be used with eggs, as a sandwich patty, or for a main dish. If serving them for a main dish, you might want to make Creole Sauce (see Creole Cabbage, page 67) to top them.

1 cup lentils	½ teaspoon rubbed sage
2 cups water	¼ teaspoon allspice
1 large egg	¼ teaspoon ground black pepper
¼ cup milk	¼ cup unsifted all-purpose flour
1 cup Grape Nuts	Bacon fat or vegetable shortening for
2 tablespoons finely chopped onion	frying
1 teaspoon salt	

Cook lentils in water until tender and all water has evaporated—35 to 40 minutes.

Meanwhile, beat together egg and milk. Stir in Grape Nuts, onion, salt, sage, allspice, and pepper.

When lentils are tender, fold into cereal mixture. Divide into 12 portions on wax paper; pat each into a 3-inch round and coat with flour.

Heat bacon fat or shortening in a large skillet. Fry patties until brown on both sides and serve.

12 Patties

HAM LOAF WITH MOLASSES

★ ★

Corn flakes contribute vitamin B and the molasses adds some iron to this easy-to-make loaf. This is a thrifty way to use the leftovers from a holiday ham and the chilled leftovers from the loaf make an excellent luncheon meat for sandwiches the next day.

¾ cup corn flakes, crumbled

½ cup milk

1 large egg

2 tablespoons molasses

¼ teaspoon ground cloves

¾ pound ground ham

½ pound ground pork

Combine corn flakes, milk, egg, molasses, and cloves in a medium bowl. Set aside 5 minutes.

Preheat oven to 350°F. Grease an 8-inch loaf pan.

Add ham and pork to corn flake mixture and stir with a fork until combined; pack into greased pan.

Bake until a meat thermometer inserted in center of loaf registers 170°F—50 to 55 minutes. Cool in pan 5 minutes. Carefully remove to serving platter and serve immediately or cool 20 minutes, cover, and refrigerate to serve cold.

6 Servings

"Good nutrition doesn't depend upon the amount of money you have to spend on food. 'Good food'—'the right kinds of food for building and maintaining health'—doesn't necessarily mean expensive food. On the contrary, many low-cost, plain foods are often richer in nutritive value than more expensive foods."—*Eating for Fitness: Home Volunteers Guide to Better Nutrition*, 1943

MOLASSES RYE BREAD

★ ★

Rye bread needs a bit of sweetness and molasses was the perfect iron-rich, ration point–free choice. Although everyone was very busy, the number of yeast bread recipes published leads me to believe that homemade bread was still important enough to homemakers that they found the time to make it for their families.

1 cup milk	1 package active dry yeast
¼ cup molasses	1 large egg, lightly beaten
¼ cup vegetable shortening or butter (or a mixture)	3 to 3½ cups unsifted all-purpose flour
¾ teaspoon salt	1 cup unsifted rye flour
¼ cup warm (105° to 110°F) water	

Heat milk in a small saucepan over medium heat until bubbles form at edge of pan; stir in molasses, shortening, and salt. Pour mixture into a large bowl; set aside to cool to between 105° and 110°F.

Meanwhile, combine warm water and yeast in a cup and set aside for yeast to soften.

When milk mixture has cooled, beat in egg and yeast mixture. Add 3 cups all-purpose flour and the rye flour; stir until a soft dough forms.

Turn dough out onto a work surface sprinkled with some of remaining ½ cup all-purpose flour. Knead 5 minutes, adding as much flour as necessary to make dough manageable. Place dough in a greased bowl, cover, and set aside in a warm place until double in size—about 1 hour.

Grease an oval in center of a baking sheet. Shape dough into an oval loaf and place on greased pan. Set aside in a warm place until double in size—about 45 minutes.

Preheat oven to 400°F. Bake bread 15 minutes; reduce heat to 350°F and bake until golden brown and loaf sounds hollow when tapped on the top—20 to 25 minutes longer. Cool at least 30 minutes before slicing.

4 Servings

3

CULTIVATE AND CAN

★★★★★★★★★★★★★★★★★★★★★

Beet Relish

Creole Cabbage

Green-Tomato Mincemeat Pie

Harvard Beets

Canned Green-Tomato Relish

Scalloped Spinach and Tomatoes

Pear Butter

Six-Layer Dinner

Quick Chili Sauce

Swiss Chard

Hot Cabbage Slaw

Vegetable Rarebit on Toast

Snap-Bean Salad

Victory Pancakes

Summer Lettuce Salad

Victory Vegetable Plate

Corn Fritters

The Old Way

. . . there are four different ways of canning:

1. Open kettle method for fruits and tomatoes; prepared fruit or tomatoes are filled hot into sterilized jars, and hermetically sealed.

2. Cold pack for fruits, tomatoes, etc.; prepared fruit or tomatoes are placed in sterilized jars, covered with hot water or syrup, processed at boiling point half-closed, and hermetically sealed.

3. Hot pack for fruits and tomatoes; prepared fruit or tomatoes are filled into sterilized jars, processed at boiling point, and tightly sealed.

4. Meats and nonacid vegetables, processed in steam pressure canner above 212°F.—*Home Canning for Victory: Pickling, Preserving, Dehydrating,* 1942

The New Way

There are only two processing methods recommended for the home canning of foods . . .

Boiling-Water Method—Acid foods are processed in a boiling-water canner. . . . A temperature of 212°F is reached and must be maintained for the time specified by the recipe.

Steam-Pressure Method—Low-acid foods must be processed in a steam-pressure canner. In order to destroy all bacteria, their spores and the toxins they produce, low-acid foods must be superheated to a temperature of 240°F and held there for the time specified by the recipe."—*Ball Blue Book: Guide to Home Canning, Freezing & Dehydration,* 1997

When reminiscing, the first thing women who managed a home during the war years remember is their Victory Garden. The joy of producing and preserving their own food was an experience they never forgot. As a matter of fact, most of them continued to grow a vegetable garden and to can its bounty for many years to come.

Backyard gardens were encouraged during World War I and continued through the Depression as a way of supplementing the family food supply. When the National Victory Garden Program was announced at the end of December 1941, increasing production in time for the 1942 season was not a problem. It was also a program that everyone could be involved in together, no matter their age or gender. By 1943, America had taken on the responsibility of feeding our European allies. This and the need for canned products to feed the U.S. troops, led to shortages and eventually rationing of commercially canned fruits and vegetables. The government announced that although the 1942 harvest was a big success, Victory Gardeners were to plant, harvest, and can even more in 1943. But they needn't have worried. The Victory Garden and home-canning programs were so popular and successful that by the summer of '43, the peak of Victory Garden activity, there were nearly 20 million Victory Gardens in America and they produced a third of all vegetables used. In December of that year, the War Food Administration announced that "American pantries are bulging with the largest stocks of canned goods in history." My mother exemplifies the energy with which homemakers followed the government's call to can as she proudly remembers that by the fall of 1943 she had over 600 jars of food in her basement that she had "put up" with no one else to help. This must have been some of the activity I remember in our wartime kitchen.

While the gardening seemed to work without a hitch, the canning process provided some difficulties. Because canning was the number-one choice for preserving the Victory Garden, equipment became scarce. Home canners were encouraged to form cooperative groups to share both equipment and labor. Canning centers were set up in many towns where women could come and use pressure canners to "put up" meats and nonacid vegetables. It was big news when the March 1944 issue of *American Cookery* reported that "the War Production Board has released half a million canners for home use—good news to the housewife. These canners are made of enamel and in one size—seven quart or nine pint capacity to be used for the water bath method of canning acid fruits and vegetables." The large numbers of inexperienced canners working with less than ideal equipment because of the shortages opened the possibility for disaster. Directions for safe canning were in every magazine along with headline warnings about the dangers of botulism. Government bulletins reminded canners that all nonacid vegetables and meats *must* be canned in a pressure canner, that oven canning was risky, and that all home-canned vegetables should be cooked for fifteen minutes before they were tasted even if they had been canned under pressure.

Home-front cooks heeded the warnings and found the experience so rewarding that they became reluctant to use up the stores they had worked so hard producing. Soon magazine articles were telling them, "Don't Hoard Your Home-Canned Foods," "Eat It—Don't Save It!" *Good Housekeeping* magazine warned, "There are two mistakes you can make in using your home-canned foods. The first—serving favorites too often. The second—using your supply so sparingly that you'll have some left over when the summer's garden crop comes along." Menus appeared using the home-canned sauces and condiments such as Beet Relish, Canned Green-Tomato Relish, and Quick Chili Sauce as accompaniments. Articles showed colorful jars of corn, beets, spinach, tomatoes, green beans, and cabbage, coming to the table as Corn Fritters, Creole Cabbage, Harvard Beets, Scalloped Spinach and Tomatoes, or Snap-Bean Salad.

Dehydration and freezing were explored as additional ways of food preservation. Commercial dehydration facilities experimented on a wide variety of products. While only dried vegetables for soup mixes and a brief flurry of pumpkin and cranberry flakes for the holidays were available for home use, these facilities produced dehydrated vegetables, fruits, juices, milk, and meat as well as the infamous powdered eggs for the armed services and our Allies abroad. The advantages of reduced perishability and greatly reduced volume and weight made them invaluable in the effort to get as much food as possible to the war front quickly. Home dehydrators were just coming on the market, but were not known to be very reliable. Most home drying was done by old-fashioned methods. Our family dried corn and green beans in trays on a kerosene stove in the backyard, and my aunt was able to make very good dried apples using the heat from the pilot of her gas stove. But home drying was never an important alternative to canning.

Clarence Birdseye's frozen foods had been available on the consumer market since 1930, but home refrigerators had very little freezer space and most families reserved that for ice cubes and ice cream. Families that did want to freeze food or buy and store frozen food had to rent space at a frozen-food locker plant. When they wanted to use a box of frozen food they had to drive to the locker plant during business hours and take a package out of their locker. Although the frozen foods were a lot more like fresh foods than their canned counterparts, the system was not very convenient. It was not until home freezers and refrigerators with large freezer sections arrived in the 1950s that freezing became an option for most families. The concept of using frozen food was still so unusual in the early 1940s that a *Good Housekeeping* article took the space to answer the question, "What are frozen foods?"

Times have changed and so has preserving (see box on page 52). People don't just can to save things for the winter anymore; if they are going to that bother, they want to have a unique product that will add an exciting touch to a dish or serve as a special homemade present for a friend. The first group of recipes in this chapter fit that description. The remaining dishes are old-fashioned vegetable recipes, some using produce fresh from the Victory Garden and some that might be made with home- or commercially canned vegetables.

Getting Ready to Can

These days all products that will be jarred and stored at room temperature must be processed in some way. Here's how to get started:

1. Purchase new replacement lids. Wash all jars and bands.

2. Shortly before food is ready for processing, place jars and bands in a large kettle and cover with water. Heat to a boil and boil rapidly 10 minutes. Do not remove from water until ready to fill.

3. Heat replacement lids and water to cover to a boil in a small saucepan. Simmer 10 minutes. Do not remove from water until ready to use.

4. Fill and seal jars leaving 1-inch headroom for low-acid vegetables and meat, ½-inch headroom for fruit and tomatoes, and ¼-inch headroom for jellies, pickles, and relishes.

5. Process using the method and time specified in your recipe. If using a water bath canner, place jars in a canning rack and lower into kettle of boiling water. Add additional boiling water, if necessary, to cover lids by 2 inches. If using a pressure canner, follow manufacturer's directions.

6. After processing, cool jars to room temperature; label and store in a cool dry place. If any do not seal, use immediately or reprocess with new jars and lids.

BEET RELISH

★ ★

This beautiful relish makes a good accompaniment to meat loaves and main-dish casseroles. It's also good on sandwiches or as a salad dressing on assorted greens.

3 cups cider vinegar	4 cups finely chopped peeled beets,
1½ cups packed light brown sugar	either raw or cooked
¼ teaspoon celery seed	2 cups finely chopped cabbage
¼ teaspoon mustard seed	2 cups finely chopped celery
¼ teaspoon salt	2 cups finely chopped onions
¼ teaspoon red pepper flakes	2 cups finely chopped red bell peppers

Bring vinegar, brown sugar, celery seed, mustard seed, salt, and red pepper flakes to a boil in a large nonaluminum saucepan. Stir in beets, cabbage, celery, onions, and bell peppers. Return to a boil; reduce heat to low and simmer, uncovered, 20 minutes.

Meanwhile, sterilize jars and prepare equipment for processing relish (see page 55).

When relish has cooked, pack into jars; seal and process 15 minutes in boiling water bath canner (see page 55). Cool to room temperature. Check seal, label, and store. Use within 1 year.

5 to 6 Pints

"Mother tells the story of Dad's letter from France requesting a chicken. So Mom prepared and canned a chicken in a glass jar and sent it off to Dad. Meanwhile he was sent to Camp Kilmer, New Jersey, for treatment of an injury. He arrived back home in Middletown when the chicken finally caught up to him. So together, Mom and Dad enjoyed the chicken that had traveled half way around the world." *Julie A. Lenard, Middletown, Pennsylvania, telling the story of her mother, Martha Tittiger*

GREEN-TOMATO MINCEMEAT PIE

★ ★

The spicy filling for this pie can be made ahead and canned, but I have never had enough green tomatoes at a time to make more than one pie. My grandmother used to make this pie when Grandpa brought in all the tomatoes left on the vines because the first frost was threatening.

2 pounds green tomatoes, unpeeled
  and coarsely chopped

1 pound apples, peeled and chopped

1 cup dark seedless raisins

1 tablespoon grated lemon peel

1 cup packed light brown sugar

½ cup cider vinegar

½ cup cold water

2 teaspoons ground cinnamon

¼ teaspoon salt

¼ teaspoon ground allspice

¼ teaspoon ground cloves

1 recipe Flaky Pastry (page 211)

Combine tomatoes, apples, raisins, lemon peel, brown sugar, vinegar, water, cinnamon, salt, allspice, and cloves in a large nonaluminum kettle. Bring mixture to a boil over high heat, stirring constantly. Reduce heat to low and simmer, uncovered, stirring frequently until tomatoes and apples are tender and mixture has thickened—about 45 minutes. Meanwhile, prepare pastry.

Preheat oven to 375°F. Roll out half of dough to an 11-inch round. Transfer to a 9-inch pie plate; fill with mincemeat. Moisten edge of pastry. Roll out remaining half of dough to a 10-inch round. Cut a hole in the center and place over filling. Turn excess pastry under and flute edges. Place pie on rimmed baking sheet.

Bake pie until crust is golden and filling bubbles through center hole, about 45 minutes. Cool 30 minutes before cutting. Serve slightly warm.

4 Servings

CANNED GREEN-TOMATO RELISH

★ ★

Also called piccalilli, this sweet and sour condiment is a traditional accompaniment to cooked meats and a delicious addition to cold meat sandwiches. Home Canning for Victory, *published in 1942, says, "this is one of the oldest of mixed, chopped pickles and there are many variations as to ingredients and seasonings."*

4 cups chopped green tomatoes	1½ cups cider vinegar
1 cup chopped firm red tomatoes	1 cup packed light brown sugar
2 cups chopped red bell peppers	1 teaspoon mustard seed
2 cups chopped green cabbage	¼ to ½ teaspoon hot red pepper
¼ cup salt	(cayenne)

The day before canning, combine green and red tomatoes, peppers, cabbage, and salt in a nonmetal kettle or large bowl. Cover and refrigerate overnight.

The next day, drain vegetables very well, discarding liquid. Rinse and drain again. Bring vinegar, brown sugar, mustard seed, and red pepper to a boil in a 5-quart enameled saucepan. Stir in vegetables and simmer 20 minutes.

Meanwhile, sterilize jars and prepare equipment for processing relish (see page 55).

When relish has cooked, pack into jars; seal and process 15 minutes in boiling water bath canner (see page 55). Cool to room temperature. Check seal, label, and store. Use within 1 year.

3 to 4 Pints

WARTIME SPECIAL

Cream of Tomato Soup

⅓ cup butter

¼ cup flour

3 cups tomato juice

¼ teaspoon baking soda

3 cups milk

1 tablespoon sugar

1 teaspoon salt

2 tablespoons crumbled
  Roquefort cheese

Melt butter; blend in flour until smooth. Pour in tomato juice and stir until it thickens. Add soda, then milk, sugar, and salt. Heat thoroughly. Divide into bowls and top with cheese. This soup does not curdle.

"Dad and I had such a huge garden, apple trees, and rhubarb patch, that the vegetables, fruits, sauerkraut, dill pickles, jams, jellies, fried chicken, meat balls, soups, catsup, chow-chow that I canned the autumn of 1943 kept Dad, my little son, and myself in those foods through 1947! Our fresh potatoes saw us through 1945." *Eve Veerkamp, Challenge, California*

PEAR BUTTER

Although I always start with the same weight of fruit when making pear or apple butter, I never come out with exactly the same amount of pulp, because some fruits are juicier than others. That's why the old fruit butter recipes call for measuring the pulp and then adding half that measure of sugar. This wartime recipe uses half brown sugar with delicious results.

10 ripe pears (6 pounds)	**½ cup orange juice**
½ cup granulated sugar	**½ teaspoon ground cinnamon**
½ cup packed light brown sugar	

Peel, core, and coarsely chop pears. Place in a heavy 5-quart saucepan or Dutch oven. Cover and cook over low heat, stirring frequently, until pears release liquid and soften into a pulp—about 10 minutes. Uncover and continue to cook, stirring frequently until pulp is thick and no juice is visible at edge of pan. (For a very smooth butter, puree pulp with a food mill or processor at this point.) Pulp should measure about 2 cups.

Combine pulp, granulated and brown sugars, orange juice, and cinnamon in same saucepan and continue to cook over low heat, stirring frequently until mixture is very thick, about 20 minutes.

Meanwhile, sterilize 1 pint or 2 half-pint jars and prepare equipment for processing butter (see page 55).

Transfer to a sterilized jar or jars leaving ¼-inch headroom; seal and process 15 minutes in boiling water bath canner (see page 55). Cool to room temperature. Check seal, label, and store. Use within 1 year.

1 Pint

"I learned the hard way all right!—and believe me, since I put up fruit of my own I appreciate Del Monte quality more than ever!"—Del Monte *advertisement, 1943*

QUICK CHILI SAUCE

★ ★

This sauce cooks about a half hour, which is a great time savings over the traditional 2 to 3 hours. Small-batch canning is convenient when you are preserving the daily harvest from a small garden.

4 cups chopped, skinned ripe tomatoes (about 2 pounds)	¼ cup cider vinegar
½ cup finely chopped onion	¼ cup packed light brown sugar
½ cup finely chopped green bell pepper	½ teaspoon salt
	¼ teaspoon ground cloves
	¼ teaspoon ground allspice

Combine tomatoes, onion, and green pepper. Cook, stirring constantly over medium heat until liquid forms—about 5 minutes.

Stir in vinegar, brown sugar, salt, cloves, and allspice. Cook, 20 to 25 minutes or until thick and reduced to 1 pint. Spoon into a sterilized jar, cover with a sterilized lid, and refrigerate for use within a week.

To preserve for a longer period, sterilize 1 pint or 2 half-pint jars and prepare equipment for processing (see page 55).

Transfer sauce to a sterilized jar or jars leaving ¼-inch headroom; seal and process 15 minutes in boiling water bath canner (see page 55). Cool to room temperature. Check seal, label, and store. Use within 1 year.

1 Pint

"There is a military, scientific precision about preserving foods. The rules are simple and clear cut, but there must be no 'cutting of corners.' . . . Only ignorance and carelessness bring danger. Follow directions carefully, just as you would your knitting recipes, and all will be well."—*Home Canning for Victory: Pickling, Preserving, Dehydrating, 1942*

HOT CABBAGE SLAW

Cabbage was one of the most successful crops in Victory Gardens across America, and many cabbage recipes appeared in fall and winter magazines during the war years. This can be served as a side dish or in place of a salad.

1 small head (1¼ pounds) green
   cabbage
1 large red bell pepper, stem, seeds,
   and ribs discarded
1 cup water
2 tablespoons bacon fat or vegetable
   shortening

2 tablespoons all-purpose flour
2 tablespoons lemon juice
1½ teaspoons sugar
½ teaspoon salt
¼ teaspoon ground black pepper

Rinse and shred cabbage. Thinly slice pepper lengthwise.

Combine cabbage, pepper, and water in a heavy 4-quart saucepan. Bring to a boil over medium heat. Cook 10 minutes. Pour into a colander and drain very well, reserving 1 cup liquid. If necessary, add water to liquid to make 1 cup.

In same saucepan, melt bacon fat; stir in flour until smooth. Gradually stir in 1 cup reserved vegetable liquid, the lemon juice, sugar, salt, and pepper. Bring to a boil, stirring constantly.

Stir reserved cabbage and pepper into thickened sauce and return to a boil. Cook, stirring, until vegetables reach desired tenderness, 5 to 10 minutes. Transfer to a bowl and serve.

6 Servings

SNAP-BEAN SALAD

★ ★

Sometimes there is just not enough of a prepared vegetable to fill that last quart jar. If that happens when you are canning Victory Garden snap beans, this is an excellent way to extend them with eggs to make a main-dish salad.

3 cups diagonally cut cooked green beans

⅓ cup oil and vinegar salad dressing (see page 155)

4 large hard-cooked eggs, very finely chopped

3 tablespoons mayonnaise

3 tablespoons grated horseradish

3 cups packed salad greens (rinsed, crisped, and broken into pieces)

2 whole peeled tomatoes, coarsely chopped

Marinate beans in dressing 30 minutes.

Meanwhile, combine eggs, mayonnaise, and horseradish. Arrange greens on a large platter.

When beans have marinated, drain reserving marinade. Spoon egg mixture into center of greens on platter. Arrange beans around egg mixture and tomatoes around beans. Drizzle reserved marinade over all and serve.

4 Servings

"I'd come home at five o'clock, fix my evening meal, and then I was given the pressure cooker. So I was canning until midnight and later, night after night." *Americans Remember the Home Front*, 1977

SUMMER LETTUCE SALAD

★ ★

It was always a special occasion when the garden lettuce was ready to harvest. The season always seemed so very short, and it was the only time all year that lettuce meant anything other than ice-berg from the corner store. Fresh raw peas at the beginning of the season were also a unique treat and the combination makes a salad that needs only the simplest dressing.

¼ cup light corn syrup

2 to 3 tablespoons cider vinegar, to taste

⅛ teaspoon salt

⅛ teaspoon ground black pepper

4 cups packed green leaf lettuce (rinsed, crisped, and broken into pieces

1 cup shelled fresh green peas, uncooked

Combine the syrup, vinegar, salt, and pepper in a ½-pint jar with a tight-fitting lid. Shake until all vinegar is incorporated.

Divide the lettuce onto 4 chilled luncheon plates. Top each serving with peas. Drizzle dressing over salads.

4 Servings

CORN FRITTERS

★ ★

These make a good alternate for the fried green tomatoes on the Victory Vegetable Plate (page 74). If you are serving them as the protein source in a meatless meal, you might want to use undiluted evaporated milk in place of the milk in the recipe.

1¼ cups unsifted all-purpose flour

1 teaspoon baking powder

½ teaspoon salt

2 large eggs, lightly beaten

¼ cup milk

1½ cups fresh yellow corn kernels

2 tablespoons vegetable shortening or
   bacon fat

Honey or syrup, optional

Combine flour, baking powder, and salt in medium bowl. Stir in eggs and milk just until flour mixture has all been moistened. Mixture should be lumpy. Fold in corn.

Melt 1 teaspoon shortening in a large skillet over medium heat. Drop corn batter by tablespoonfuls into skillet and fry until brown on both sides and centers feel firm when gently pressed—5 to 7 minutes. Remove to platter and keep warm. Repeat until all batter has been used, adding shortening as needed. Serve with honey or syrup, if desired.

4 Servings

> "How much fruit your family will have next winter—or how little—is entirely up to you! But remember, there are only 3 ways to get it! You'll be able to buy some in cans, but only what your ration book allows. You'll be able to buy some fresh, but only what's in season. You will be able to serve home-canned fruits and the only limit is what you yourself put up this summer."—*Del Monte advertisement, 1943*

WARTIME SPECIAL

Chicken Gumbo Soup

1 large fowl

5 quarts water

1 can tomatoes

1 large onion, chopped

4 stalks celery with leaves

2 cups okra

3 diced potatoes

1 cup rice

3 ears corn (cut from cob)

1 cup lima beans

Salt and pepper

Wash and cut up chicken. Place in water with tomatoes, onion, celery, and a teaspoon salt. Boil 2 hours. Strain soup and remove chicken. Add other vegetables and cook 30 minutes. Remove chicken from bones and add to soup. Season to taste and can.

"I went to R. H. Macy's in New York and bought a Burpee pressure cooker which I use to this day. I canned fruits and vegetables which I bought fresh at the pushcarts; in those days nothing was frozen." *Edith Hohman, Fort Ann, New York*

CREOLE CABBAGE

★ ★

Creole sauce was a favorite during the early 1940s. It was used with everything from seafood to poultry to vegetables. This could easily be turned into a main dish with the addition of a little left-over ham.

2 tablespoons bacon fat or shortening	Salt
¾ cup thinly sliced onion	2 whole cloves
½ cup thinly sliced green bell pepper	1 clove garlic
1 pint home-canned or 1	1 bay leaf
(15-ounce) can tomatoes	1 medium head (2 pounds) green
1½ teaspoons brown sugar	cabbage, coarsely grated

In a heavy skillet, over medium heat, melt bacon fat or shortening. Add onion and pepper; sauté until onion is golden.

Stir tomatoes, brown sugar, and ¼ teaspoon salt into onion mixture and bring to a boil over medium heat. Insert cloves into garlic and add to tomato mixture along with bay leaf; simmer, uncovered, stirring occasionally, 15 minutes.

Meanwhile, cook cabbage in 1-inch boiling salted water in large, covered saucepan, until just tender. Drain well and return to saucepan. Discard garlic clove and bay leaf; pour sauce over cabbage, and toss to combine. Transfer to a serving bowl and serve hot.

4 Servings

HARVARD BEETS

★ ★

This traditional preparation is often the only way children will eat beets. A February 1942 Good Housekeeping *article about family members taking over the cooking while Mother was working or doing community service tells of a young boy making this because it was a favorite at the summer camp he attended.*

¼ cup sugar	¼ cup water or liquid from canned beets
1 tablespoon cornstarch	3 cups diced cooked or canned beets
¼ teaspoon salt	1 tablespoon butter or margarine
¼ cup cider vinegar	1 teaspoon minced onion

Blend sugar, cornstarch, and salt in a heavy 2-quart saucepan, or top of a double boiler. Gradually stir in vinegar and water; cook over low heat or, if using double boiler, over boiling water, until thickened and smooth.

Stir in beets, butter, and onion and cook gently 15 minutes.

6 Servings

"Despite the wonderful mass production by the commercial canners, the smaller supplies that cannot get to market, when multiplied by the efforts of forty-five million women, will be a notable addition to the winter food supply, and will release just that much more to feed starving nations and our own men bearing arms in the far corners of the world."
—*Home Canning for Victory: Pickling, Preserving, Dehydrating,* 1942

SCALLOPED SPINACH AND TOMATOES

★ ★

This recipe makes a main dish from two Victory Garden favorites. Although washing fresh garden spinach is more work, there is no match for the resulting fresh flavor.

3 pounds fresh spinach, rinsed and chopped, or 2 (10-ounce) packages frozen chopped spinach

Salt

2 tablespoons vegetable shortening or butter (or a mixture)

¼ cup finely chopped onion

2 tablespoons flour

¼ teaspoon ground black pepper

½ cup milk

4 medium tomatoes, thinly sliced

1 cup fresh bread crumbs

1 tablespoon butter, melted

½ cup grated Cheddar or American cheese

Cook spinach in 1 inch boiling salted water until just wilted. Drain very well.

Meanwhile, melt shortening in heavy medium skillet. Add onion and sauté until golden. Stir in flour, ½ teaspoon salt, and the pepper until smooth. Very gradually stir in milk; cook over low heat, stirring constantly until sauce has thickened. Fold in spinach.

Preheat oven to 350°F. Generously grease a shallow 1½-quart baking dish. Pour half of spinach mixture into dish in an even layer; top with half of tomatoes. Repeat layering with remaining spinach and tomatoes. Combine crumbs and butter. Sprinkle crumb mixture and cheese over top of tomatoes.

Place on rimmed baking sheet and bake 30 to 35 minutes or until browned and bubbly.

4 Servings

SIX-LAYER DINNER

★ ★

An abundance of fresh-from-the-garden vegetables extends the layer of ground beef into a hearty meal.

1 tablespoon flour	¾ pound ground beef
¾ teaspoon salt	1 cup thinly sliced raw onions
¼ teaspoon ground black pepper	1 cup thinly sliced green bell peppers
2 cups sliced raw potatoes	2 cups chopped ripe tomatoes, see
2 cups thinly sliced celery	Note

Preheat oven to 350°F. Grease a shallow 2-quart casserole. Combine flour, salt, and black pepper in a custard cup.

Layer potatoes, celery, ground beef, onions, bell peppers, and tomatoes in order in greased casserole, sprinkling each layer with a sixth of the flour mixture.

Bake until the potatoes are tender, 1 to 1¼ hours. Serve from the casserole.

4 to 6 Servings

NOTE: Or use chopped, well-drained canned tomatoes and be sure to save the juice for another use.

Toward the end of the war, so many farm workers were on active duty that women, children, and retired workers were encouraged to volunteer for the Crop Corps during the harvest season. A Dole ad thanks the men, women, boys, and girls of Hawaii for harvesting a "splendid crop of Dole Pineapple." The March 1944 issue of *American Cookery* notes that that year, "all women and girls who aid the war effort in the production of food, feed and fiber may wear the trim comfortable uniform until now worn only by the Women's Land Army." The uniform costs $6.20 and is described as a light blue cotton shirt, navy cotton twill overalls, and a cap.

SWISS CHARD

★ ★

One of the joys of gardening is experiencing vegetables that are not regularly found in the market. Swiss chard thrives in much of this country and must have been found in many Victory Gardens because magazines ran a variety of recipes that featured it.

½ teaspoon salt

2 pounds Swiss chard

4 teaspoons melted margarine or butter

⅛ teaspoon pepper

1 tablespoon vinegar or lemon juice

Bring 2 inches water and the salt to a boil in a large heavy saucepan. Rinse chard; separate stems from leaves. Cut stems into 2-inch pieces; cut leaves crosswise into 1-inch strips.

Add stems to boiling water; cook until tender—about 10 minutes. Remove from water with a slotted spoon and keep warm. Add leaves to boiling water; cook 5 minutes. Drain leaves very well and toss with 2 teaspoons margarine and the pepper. Mound in center of serving plate. Drain stems well and toss with remaining 2 teaspoons margarine. Arrange around edge of plate. Drizzle with vinegar or lemon juice and serve.

4 Servings

"To put it bluntly, most of us are going to be lucky to get a salad, these days. For the duration, we may as well make up our minds to say goodbye to many of the succulent salads we used to enjoy, for one of the casualties of war on the home-food-front is the salad."—*Successful Salads: How to Make and Use Them During Rationing and Wartime Food Scarcities*, 1943

VEGETABLE RAREBIT ON TOAST

★ ★

This nourishing dish is an excellent way to use up a mixture of already cooked, fresh or canned vegetables.

2 tablespoons vegetable shortening or
  bacon fat, see Note
3 tablespoons all-purpose flour
½ teaspoon dry mustard
¼ teaspoon salt
1½ cups milk
1 teaspoon Worcestershire sauce

1½ cups grated Cheddar cheese
2 cups mixed cooked vegetables
½ cup chopped fresh or well-drained
  canned tomatoes
6 thick slices whole-wheat or white
  bread

Melt shortening in top of a double boiler, over very low direct heat. Stir in flour, mustard, and salt, until smooth. Very gradually stir in milk and Worcestershire sauce. Cook, stirring constantly until thickened.

Fold cheese, vegetables and tomatoes into sauce. Set pan into bottom of double boiler over boiling water and cook, covered, 10 minutes.

Meanwhile, toast bread and place on dinner plates. Divide rarebit onto pieces of toast and serve.

6 Servings

NOTE: Reduce salt to ⅛ teaspoon if using bacon fat.

> "To the many high school students who pitched in to help pick and pack the 1944 food crop, all America joins in saying 'Thanks.' "—*Campbell's Tomato Soup advertisement, November 1944*

VICTORY PANCAKES

★ ★

Just step out to the Victory Garden and pick a nutritious variety of vegetables for these lunch or supper pancakes. The addition of a cheese sauce makes it a main dish.

Pancakes:

1 cup unsifted all-purpose
   flour

1 teaspoon baking powder

½ teaspoon salt

¼ teaspoon ground black pepper

1 cup packed very thinly sliced
   fresh spinach

1 cup packed very thinly sliced lettuce

1 cup grated carrots

1 cup grated potatoes

¼ cup grated onion

2 large eggs, lightly beaten

Vegetable shortening for frying

Cheese Sauce:

2 tablespoons cornstarch

1 teaspoon dry mustard

¾ teaspoon onion salt

2 cups milk

½ cup grated Cheddar cheese

Heat oven to 200°F. Combine flour, baking powder, salt, and pepper in a small bowl or on wax paper.

Combine spinach, lettuce, carrots, potatoes, and onion in a large bowl. Stir in dry ingredients and eggs just until combined.

Melt some shortening in a large heavy skillet or on a griddle. Drop about ¼ cup vegetable mixture into skillet and spread to make a 3½-inch pancake; repeat to make as many as can fit easily in skillet. Fry until golden brown on each side. Remove pancakes to a baking sheet and keep warm in the oven until all have been fried.

Meanwhile, make cheese sauce. Combine cornstarch, mustard, and onion salt in a heavy 2-quart saucepan; gradually stir in milk. Bring to a boil over low heat, stirring occasionally until thickened. Stir in cheese and keep warm until ready to serve with pancakes.

12 Pancakes

VICTORY VEGETABLE PLATE

★ ★

Dozens of recipes appeared with Victory in their name. This colorful arrangement of vegetables featured the bounty of early summer Victory Gardens. One of the conveniences of having your own tomato plants is being able to have green tomatoes whenever you want them.

1 pound green or firm red tomatoes
¼ cup all-purpose flour
1 large egg, lightly beaten
⅓ cup dry bread crumbs
¾ teaspoon salt
¼ teaspoon ground black pepper
¼ teaspoon dried thyme leaves
2 tablespoons bacon fat or vegetable shortening

12 stalks asparagus (12 ounces), sliced diagonally ½ inch thick
6 medium carrots (12 ounces), peeled and sliced diagonally ¼ inch thick
2 teaspoon lemon juice
2 teaspoons melted butter
1 teaspoon light brown sugar

Slice tomatoes and dip first in flour, then in egg, and finally in a mixture of crumbs, ¼ teaspoon salt, pepper, and thyme.

Heat 1 tablespoon bacon fat in large skillet. Fry tomatoes until brown on all sides adding more fat as needed. Remove and drain well. Keep warm until all have been cooked.

Meanwhile, cook asparagus in water to cover in a small saucepan until just tender, about 5 minutes. Cook carrots in water to cover in another small saucepan until tender, about 7 minutes.

Arrange fried tomatoes in center of a large platter. Drain asparagus very well; toss with the lemon juice, 1 teaspoon butter, and another ¼ teaspoon salt. Spoon at one end of the platter. Drain carrots very well; toss with sugar, remaining 1 teaspoon butter, and remaining ¼ teaspoon salt. Spoon at the other end of the platter and serve.

4 Servings

4

SWEET SACRIFICE

★ ★ ★ ★ ★ ★ ★ ★ ★ ★ ★ ★ ★ ★ ★ ★ ★ ★ ★ ★

Brown Sugar Doughnuts

Oatmeal Muffins

Vermont Johnny Cake

Honey Marshmallow Custard

Maple Tapioca

Pineapple Delight

Graham Cracker Ice Cream

Sugarless Fresh Berry Ice Cream

Log Cabin Pudding

Victory Pudding

"Sugarless" Brownies

Honey Apple Pie in Oatmeal Crust

Maple Custard Pie

Sugarless Two-Egg Cake

Molasses Whole-Wheat Cake

Chocolate-Condensed Milk Frosting

Sugarless Boiled Frosting

When a Recipe Calls for 1 cup Granulated Sugar You May Substitute:

Molasses—1 cup plus ½ teaspoon baking soda for each cup
Maple Syrup—1¼ cups plus ¼ teaspoon baking soda for each cup; reduce liquid by ½
Honey—1 cup plus ⅛ teaspoon baking soda for each cup; reduce liquid by ¼
Corn Syrup—1 cup plus ⅛ teaspoon baking soda for each cup; reduce liquid by ⅓

For comparable sweetness you would need 1½ cups molasses or maple syrup, ¾ cup honey or 2 cups corn syrup to replace each cup of sugar.—*American Cookery*, March 1942

Sugar was one of the first food items to be rationed. Government officials explained that the shortage of sugar was due to the loss of the cane fields in the Philippines as well as the reassignment of ocean transport at home, and spoke for the nation by saying that, "rather than have an abundance of sugar, Americans preferred to reduce consumption, provide for a good margin of safety in stocks in this country, ration the reduced supply equitably and systematically—and fight the war." The ships that had been used to transport sugar from the Caribbean islands were now transporting wartime materials, and no change was in sight, so on May 5, 1942, "the Sugar Book" became the only legal way to get refined granulated sugar from the grocer. As part of the Uniform Coupon Rationing program, the books gave everyone the same number of stamps. At first sugar was available so that everyone could have a half-pound per person per week. Soon supplies dwindled and the stamps were validated only when sugar was available, so that everyone could buy the specified amount of sugar per stamp.

Everyone talked about the rationing, but America never gave up its sweet tooth. Other unrationed sources of sweetness such as molasses, honey, maple syrup, corn syrup, and the sugar that was a part of commercial products such as sweetened condensed milk, gelatin and pudding mixes, and sodas were used in place of granulated sugar. Because of frequent shortages of refined sugar, the less expensive brown sugar was often substituted in recipes. Homemakers were frustrated by the coarser texture and reduced sweetness of many of the products made with sugar substitutes. The government was in no way as restrictive with commercial bakers as they were with homemakers. Legions of women wrote to Washington complaining that the male bakers got tremendous consignments of sugar while the home cook could have little, forcing her to buy desserts from the very people who were getting the sugar she would have liked to have. Homemakers who wished to can fruit, jellies, and relishes could apply to local boards for ten to twenty pounds of additional sugar. But there were problems with that program too, and the sugar ran out before everyone who had applied got her allotment.

Most of the women I talked to about the sugar problem during World War II seemed to feel that it was a challenge, but not a hardship, to find ways to produce desserts that their families would like within the confines of sugar rationing. They were proud of how they coped and had positive memories of the occasions for which they created something remarkable. Their only negative memories were of the time it took waiting in lines and going from store to store to get the sugar they were entitled to. Most remembered that sugar was saved for special occasions and that members of a family would put their sugar together to bake wedding cakes, traditional holiday cookies, or treats for their boys overseas. The recipes in this chapter use very little white granulated sugar, yet all are deliciously sweet, full of flavor, and easy-to-make for cooks on a busy schedule.

Jams and Fruit Butters

BROWN SUGAR DOUGHNUTS

★ ★

Homemade doughnuts for breakfast were not considered an unusual thing in the 1940s. My grandmother and my father's sisters almost always had a big tin of fresh doughnuts on top of the refrigerator.

2 cups unsifted all-purpose flour

⅓ cup packed brown sugar

4 teaspoons baking powder

½ teaspoon salt

¼ teaspoon ground nutmeg

¼ cup vegetable shortening or butter
   (or a mixture)

½ cup milk

1 large egg, lightly beaten

Vegetable shortening or oil for deep
   frying

Confectioners' sugar

Combine flour, brown sugar, baking powder, salt, and nutmeg in a medium bowl. Add shortening and cut into flour mixture with pastry blender or 2 knives to make coarse crumbs.

Add milk and egg; stir together until a stiff dough forms. Pat out to ½-inch thickness on a floured board. Cut with doughnut cutter. Pat together scraps and continue cutting doughnuts until all dough has been used. Remove holes from doughnuts.

Heat shortening or oil to 375°F. Fry doughnuts and holes until golden on both sides. Drain on paper towels.

Put confectioners' sugar in a paper bag. Shake hot doughnuts and holes in sugar to coat completely.

18 Doughnuts, 18 Holes

OATMEAL MUFFINS

★ ★

Corn syrup replaces part of the sugar in these hearty muffins. The addition of vitamin-rich oatmeal and raisins made these perfect to pick up for a busy-day breakfast on the run.

1½ cups unsifted all-purpose flour	½ cup milk
¾ cup old-fashioned rolled oats	½ cup light corn syrup
2 tablespoons light brown sugar	1 large egg, lightly beaten
4 teaspoons baking powder	¼ cup melted shortening
1 teaspoon ground cinnamon	½ cup dark seedless raisins or
½ teaspoon salt	chopped dates

Heat oven to 400°F. Grease a 12-cup muffin pan.

Combine flour, rolled oats, brown sugar, baking powder, cinnamon, and salt in a medium bowl. Beat together milk, syrup, and egg in a small bowl.

Make a well in center of flour mixture. Add milk mixture and shortening. Stir just until all dry ingredients have been moistened. Do not overbeat. Fold in raisins.

Divide muffin mixture into greased muffin cups and bake 25 to 30 minutes or until a toothpick inserted in center of one comes out clean. Cool in pan 5 minutes. Remove to serving container and serve warm.

12 Servings

VERMONT JOHNNY CAKES

Maple syrup–sweetened baked goods were very popular during the war. The syrup in these sugar-less corn muffins helps to keep them moist in addition to adding sweetness and flavor.

1 cup unsifted all-purpose flour	½ cup milk
¾ cup cornmeal	⅓ cup maple syrup
4 teaspoons baking powder	1 large egg, lightly beaten
½ teaspoon salt	3 tablespoons melted shortening

Heat oven to 400°F. Grease a 12-cup muffin pan.

Combine flour, cornmeal, baking powder, and salt in a medium bowl. Beat together milk, syrup, and egg in a small bowl.

Make a well in center of dry ingredients. Add milk mixture and shortening. Stir just until all dry ingredients have been moistened. Do not overbeat.

Divide muffin mixture into greased muffin cups and bake 18 to 20 minutes or until a toothpick inserted in center of one comes out clean. Cool in pan 5 minutes. Remove to serving container and serve warm.

12 Servings

"It's not so easy to figure out good desserts on a sugar ration. Yet desserts are very important: they make a family feel mellow and well-treated, and they give you a chance to use nourishing milk, eggs, fruit, and cereal in ways that everyone likes. So welcome these desserts that call for so little precious sugar."—*Recipes for Today*, 1943

HONEY MARSHMALLOW CUSTARD

★ ★

During the war, marshmallows were everyone's secret ingredient. Here they add a pocket of intense sweetness in the mildly honey-sweetened custard. Starting the custard with hot milk is a time-saver; it cuts 15 to 20 minutes from the usual 1-hour baking time for custards.

2 cups milk	3 tablespoons honey
6 marshmallows	½ teaspoon vanilla extract
3 large eggs, lightly beaten	⅛ teaspoon salt

Preheat oven to 325°F. Bring milk just to a boil over low heat, stirring occasionally.

Meanwhile, lightly grease 6 small custard cups. Set cups into a 13- by 9-inch baking dish and place a marshmallow in each cup.

Combine eggs, honey, vanilla, and salt in a 1-quart glass measuring cup or heatproof pitcher. Gradually beat hot milk into honey mixture.

Place pan with custard cups on oven rack. Divide milk mixture into custard cups. Add hot water to baking pan until it reaches 1 inch up sides of custard cups. Bake until custard is set, 40 to 45 minutes.

Cool custards to room temperature, then chill several hours before serving.

6 Servings

WARTIME SPECIAL

Whipped Honey Icing

⅔ cup honey   ⅛ teaspoon salt

2 egg whites

Bring honey just to boiling. Combine egg whites and salt; beat until stiff peaks form. Pour honey into egg whites in a thin stream, beating all the time until thick and fluffy.

"I remember long summer afternoons picking many wild blackberries that Mama would can, sometimes with sugar and sometimes without sugar, for an ample supply for the cold winter months."—*Judith B. Muhammad, Baltimore, Maryland, writing about her mother, Aurora Bransford*

MAPLE TAPIOCA

★ ★

Government nutrition advisers recommended serving mildly flavored puddings like this one as a way to ensure that children (and husbands) got enough milk in their diet each day.

3 cups milk	**⅛ teaspoon salt**
¼ cup quick-cooking tapioca	**1 large egg, separated**
¼ cup maple syrup	**½ teaspoon vanilla extract**

Combine milk, tapioca, maple syrup, and salt in a heavy 2-quart saucepan. Bring to a boil over low heat, stirring constantly.

Beat egg white until soft peaks form; set aside. Lightly beat yolk in a small bowl. Gradually beat about one third of tapioca mixture into yolk. Return yolk and tapioca mixture to saucepan of tapioca. Place over low heat and bring just to a boil.

Remove tapioca from heat. Immediately fold in beaten egg white and vanilla until well mixed. Spoon into serving dish and cool to room temperature, then chill several hours before serving.

6 Servings

"The sugar-rationing program may prove to be a blessing in disguise. For while refined sugar is packed with energy, it lacks all other food factors. Then too, many of us have been eating far too much sugar—oftentimes at the expense of an adequate daily diet which should include milk, cereals, vegetables, fruits, eggs, meat, cheese, fish, etc., which help supply the day's protein, mineral and vitamin needs."—*Easy Ways to Save Sugar: Cooking, Canning, Jelly Making with Little or No Sugar, 1942*

PINEAPPLE DELIGHT

★ ★

It is not a mistake that the cream in this recipe is whipped without sugar. All of the sugar in this sweet dessert comes from commercial products, not from the cook's rationed supply.

1 (8-ounce) can pineapple rings in
   heavy syrup
12 marshmallows
½ cup dates

12 almond macaroons
1 cup heavy cream
6 well-drained maraschino cherries
   with stems, optional

Drain pineapple rings, reserving syrup. Cut each ring into 8 wedges and combine with ¼ cup syrup from can in a medium bowl. Reserve remaining syrup for another use. Quarter marshmallows and dates with a moistened scissors and add to pineapple. Crumble macaroons into mixture and stir to combine. Cover and refrigerate 1 hour.

When pineapple mixture has chilled, whip cream until stiff peaks form. Gently fold cream into pineapple mixture and transfer to a serving bowl. Cover and refrigerate at least 4 hours before serving. Arrange cherries on top just before serving, if desired.

6 Servings

GRAHAM CRACKER ICE CREAM

★ ★

The graham cracker crumbs add a bit of sweetness as well as texture to this unusual ice cream. Known to be nutritious, graham crackers added to the perception of this as a healthful dessert. It used to be necessary to give up the ice cube section of the refrigerator for a while if you wanted to make ice cream without an old-fashioned, hand-cranked, back-porch style ice cream maker. Today, the first step can be done in a baking pan in the freezer or in any kind of automatic ice cream maker.

1 cup milk	1 cup graham cracker crumbs
¼ cup honey	1 cup heavy cream, whipped
2 teaspoons vanilla extract	

Combine milk, honey, and vanilla. Freeze in ice cube trays of automatic refrigerator or in a baking pan in the freezer just until center begins to set.

Beat cubes of frozen milk mixture with electric mixer until fluffy. Fold in graham cracker crumbs and then whipped cream. Return to ice cube trays without dividers or pack into freezer containers. Freeze until solid before serving.

4 Servings

You Can Have Your Cake and Eat It, Too:

"Make smaller cakes. Use ½ or ⅓ of recipe. Make cup cakes. Serve uniced. Bake part of batter as layer or loaf . . . the other part as cup cakes. Add chocolate or spices to part of batter. Frost and use differently."—*Your Share: How to prepare appetizing, healthful meals with foods available today*, Betty Crocker 1943

SUGARLESS FRESH BERRY ICE CREAM

★ ★

This is such an easy recipe that I continue to make it even though I have several different kinds of ice cream makers around the house. The old-fashioned flavor of sweetened condensed milk peeks through the exuberance of the fresh berries. Sometimes people confuse evaporated and sweetened condensed milk these days. Look for "sweetened" on the label or you will be very disappointed with the results.

1 (14-ounce) can sweetened
   condensed milk
¼ cup fresh lemon juice
⅛ teaspoon salt

1½ cups fresh raspberries, sliced
   strawberries, blackberries, or
   blueberries
1 cup heavy cream

Combine sweetened condensed milk, lemon juice, and salt in a large bowl; set aside 5 minutes to thicken.

Meanwhile, puree berries in a blender or a food processor with a chopping blade. Strain puree and discard seeds. Beat cream in a small bowl until stiff peaks form.

When sweetened condensed milk mixture has thickened, fold in puree and then beaten cream until uniformly combined.

Pack berry ice cream into a 1½-quart freezer container and freeze at least 4 hours before serving.

6 Servings

LOG CABIN PUDDING

★ ★

The "pressure saucepan" was a popular time-saver during the war. In addition to its use in canning, it made quick dishes out of some that would normally have taken hours. This rustic pudding would need to steam at least an hour in a regular kettle but takes only 12 minutes in a pressure cooker.

1 (1-pound) loaf bread, cut into
   cubes
½ cup milk
⅓ cup molasses
3 tablespoons honey
1 tablespoon butter, melted

½ cup dark seedless raisins
½ cup water
½ cup heavy cream
1 tablespoon confectioners' sugar
½ teaspoon vanilla extract

Combine bread, milk, molasses, honey, and butter in a medium bowl. Fold in raisins. Set aside 10 minutes.

Meanwhile, select a 1½-quart pudding mold or metal bowl that will fit into your pressure cooker; grease mold well.

Spoon bread mixture into mold, cover, and place on rack in pressure cooker. Add ½ cup water to pan. Seal pan and heat to 15 pounds pressure following manufacturers' instructions. Cook 12 minutes; remove from heat and set aside until pressure subsides completely. Remove pudding from cooker; loosen edges and invert mold onto serving plate.

Whip cream with confectioners' sugar and vanilla until stiff peaks form. Serve cream with warm pudding.

4 to 6 Servings

VICTORY PUDDING

★ ★

There were many versions of Victory Pudding. They all were sweetened with molasses and included some sort of cereal. If you can find rolled wheat at a health food store, try it in this recipe. The wheat kernels remaining in the center of each flake add a delicious crunch to the pudding.

2 cups milk
⅔ cup cooked rolled wheat flakes or old-fashioned rolled oats
⅓ cup light molasses
1 large egg, lightly beaten

1 teaspoon ginger
⅛ teaspoon salt
Plain or whipped heavy cream, optional

Preheat oven to 350°F. Bring milk just to a boil in a heavy saucepan over low heat, stirring occasionally.

Meanwhile, lightly grease a 1-quart casserole or baking dish.

Combine cooked rolled wheat, molasses, egg, ginger, and salt in a heatproof bowl. Gradually beat hot milk into wheat mixture. Transfer to the casserole.

Bake until center is set, 35 to 40 minutes. Cool 20 to 30 minutes, then serve warm with cream if desired.

4 Servings

WARTIME SPECIAL

Raisin Frosting

1¼ cups raisins, ground
⅓ cup water
½ teaspoon cinnamon

⅛ teaspoon cloves
⅛ teaspoon salt

Cook all ingredients together, stirring constantly until thick. Spread over a single layer cake.

> "We still have our ration books. We couldn't afford to buy much anyway. We sold cream from our big hand-cranked separator. So we did have lots of sour cream chocolate cake and cookies."—*Mrs. Raymond Herrick, Ames, Iowa*

"SUGARLESS" BROWNIES

★ ★

Don't worry, these dark chocolate brownies aren't really "sugarless." They use a lot of corn syrup and a little brown sugar to provide the sweetness that would normally be supplied by white granulated sugar.

¾ cup light corn syrup

⅓ cup vegetable shortening or butter (or a mixture)

⅓ cup packed light brown sugar

2 (1-ounce) squares unsweetened chocolate, melted

2 large eggs

⅔ cup unsifted all-purpose flour

½ teaspoon baking powder

¼ teaspoon salt

½ teaspoon vanilla extract

½ cup chopped walnuts or pecans

Preheat oven to 350°F. Grease a 9-inch square baking pan.

Beat together syrup, shortening, brown sugar, and chocolate until fluffy. Beat in eggs one at a time.

Add flour, baking powder, and salt. Beat just until smooth. Fold in vanilla and nuts.

Spread batter into greased pan and bake 25 to 30 minutes or until a toothpick inserted in center comes out clean. Cut into 16 squares while still warm. Cool to room temperature and serve.

16 Brownies

HONEY APPLE PIE IN OATMEAL CRUST

★ ★

The use of a top-of-the-stove filling cuts the baking time from about 45 minutes for a traditional apple pie to under 15 minutes for this quick alternative.

¾ cup unsifted all-purpose flour

2 tablespoons light brown sugar

¼ teaspoon baking powder

¼ teaspoon salt

¼ cup melted vegetable shortening or butter (or a mixture)

2 tablespoons water

1 teaspoon vanilla extract

¾ cup old-fashioned rolled oats

5 large cooking apples (about 2 pounds), peeled, cored, and thinly sliced

2 tablespoons honey

2 teaspoons all-purpose flour

¼ teaspoon ground cinnamon

⅛ teaspoon ground cloves

¼ cup water

Sweetened whipped cream, optional

Preheat oven to 350°F. Generously grease an 8-inch pie plate.

Combine flour, brown sugar, baking powder, and salt in a small bowl. Stir in shortening, water, and vanilla until combined. Fold in rolled oats. Press mixture into bottom and up side (but not onto rim) of pie plate to make a crust. Bake 18 to 20 minutes until brown.

Meanwhile, in a large skillet, heat apples over low heat, stirring frequently until just tender, about 12 to 15 minutes.

Stir together honey, flour, cinnamon, and cloves; gradually stir in water and add to mixture in skillet. Bring to a boil over medium heat. Cook, stirring gently until sauce thickens. Spoon apple filling into baked crust and set aside to cool. Just before serving, top with whipped cream, if desired.

8 Servings

MAPLE CUSTARD PIE

★ ★

Fortunately, all the ingredients for this comforting pie could be found in most wartime pantries even when the ingredients for fruit pie fillings were unavailable.

4 large eggs
2 cups milk
1 cup maple syrup
¼ teaspoon salt

¼ teaspoon vegetable shortening
1 (9-inch) unbaked pastry shell with
   fluted crust

Heat oven to 350°F. Beat eggs until frothy. Gradually beat in milk, maple syrup, and salt. Spread shortening in a thin layer over bottom of pastry shell. Pour custard into pastry shell and place in center of oven.

Bake 40 to 45 minutes or until a knife inserted in center comes out clean. Cool pie to room temperature on a wire rack; then cover and refrigerate at least 2 hours before cutting.

8 Servings

Substituting Honey or Corn Syrup in Jelly Making, Jams or Preserves

"If using liquid pectin for jelly, you may substitute honey or corn syrup for part of the sugar, but only for 2 cups.

If using powdered pectin, you may substitute honey or corn syrup for one half of the total amount of the sugar.

If using no additional pectin, you may substitute honey or corn syrup for the total amount of the sugar."—*Coupon Cookery*, 1943

SUGARLESS TWO-EGG CAKE

★ ★

It is important to use cake flour for this recipe and to sift it before measuring. The recipe originally called for sifting the dry ingredients three times. This was thought to make the resulting cake lighter. Sifters with three levels of screen were available, eliminating the need to resift. Because this cake is not as sweet as cakes made with granulated sugar, it is a good choice to use for shortcakes and trifles, to fill with preserves, and to frost with sweet frostings.

2⅓ cups sifted cake flour (sift before
    measuring)

2½ teaspoons baking powder

½ teaspoon salt

½ cup vegetable shortening or butter
    (or a mixture)

1⅓ cups light corn syrup

2 large eggs

½ cup milk

3 teaspoons vanilla extract

Preheat oven to 375°F. Grease and flour two 8-inch round baking pans. Sift or stir together the flour, baking powder, and salt.

Beat the shortening in an electric mixer on high speed until fluffy; gradually beat in corn syrup. Add eggs one at a time, beating well after each addition. Add dry ingredients, milk, and vanilla; beat on low speed just until smooth.

Divide batter between prepared pans and bake 25 to 30 minutes or until centers spring back when lightly pressed. Cool layers in pans 5 minutes. Remove to wire racks and cool completely before filling and frosting.

10 Servings

MOLASSES WHOLE-WHEAT CAKE

★ ★

This molasses-sweetened cake has so much flavor that it really doesn't need frosting. Just serve it warm with a sprinkling of confectioners' sugar.

1½ cups unsifted all-purpose flour

¾ cup whole-wheat flour

1½ teaspoons baking soda

½ teaspoon salt

½ teaspoon ground nutmeg

½ teaspoon ground cloves

⅓ cup vegetable shortening or

softened butter (or a mixture)

¼ cup packed light brown sugar

⅔ cup light molasses

1 large egg

1 cup water

1 tablespoon confectioners' sugar

Preheat oven to 350°F. Grease a 9-inch square baking pan. Stir together all-purpose flour, whole-wheat flour, baking soda, salt, nutmeg, and cloves.

Beat together shortening and brown sugar until fluffy. Beat in molasses and egg. Add flour mixture to molasses mixture along with water. Beat just until smooth. Pour batter into greased pan.

Bake 30 to 35 minutes or until a toothpick inserted in center comes out clean. Cool 15 minutes; sprinkle with confectioners' sugar and cut into 12 rectangles.

12 Servings

CHOCOLATE-CONDENSED MILK FROSTING

★ ★

Sweetened condensed milk provided intense sweetness without using any of the sugar ration. This easy chocolate frosting cools with a shiny finish. We loved it on the Sugarless Two-Egg Cake.

1 (14-ounce) can sweetened
   condensed milk

3 ounces unsweetened chocolate,
   chopped
2 teaspoons vanilla extract

Combine sweetened condensed milk and chocolate in a very heavy 1-quart saucepan; bring to a boil over low heat. Cook, stirring constantly 5 minutes. Mixture should have thickened. Stir in vanilla and transfer to bowl; set aside until thick enough to spread, about 20 minutes.

Frosts and fills a 9-inch 2-layer cake

Elsie, the Borden cow, serves a frosty, milk-based drink.

SUGARLESS BOILED FROSTING

★ ★

This frosting grows from a small pan of egg whites and corn syrup to an overflowing double boiler of fluff. It beautifully fills and frosts a 9-inch cake, but is best used the day it is made. It is a testament to the haste in which weddings were planned and carried out that many of the wedding cake recipes called for this frosting.

1⅓ cups light corn syrup

2 large egg whites

⅛ teaspoon salt

2 teaspoons vanilla extract

Combine corn syrup, egg whites, and salt in top of a double boiler. Place over simmering water and beat with an electric beater until the mixture stands in stiff peaks—about 7 minutes.

Remove pan from hot water and fold in vanilla. Use to fill and frost 2 (9-inch) layers. Serve cake within 2 to 3 hours and store any leftovers in the refrigerator.

Frosts and fills a 9-inch 2-layer cake

"When topped with a fluffy meringue so ethereal
A pudding made up of the humblest cereal,
Will rate the keenest appreciation—
And lush desserts seem no longer on ration
So deck them in garnishes—the best to be mustered—
And thrill all your household with the simplest custard."
—*Food As We Like It*, 1943

5

MEAT AND MORALITY

★★★★★★★★★★★★★★★★★★★★★★★★★★

Arroz con Pato

Meat Roly Poly

Stuffed Beef Heart

Baked Meat Loaf Potatoes

Boiled Tongue with Horseradish Sauce

Beef Vegetable Burgers

Pork-U-Pines

Stuffed Peppers

Pork Chop Suey

Mother's Fried Chicken

Corn Belt Spaghetti

Curried Chicken Fricassee

Rabbit Sauté

Codfish Casserole

Spring Lamb Stew

Spanish-Style Baked Fish Fillets

Shepherd's Pie

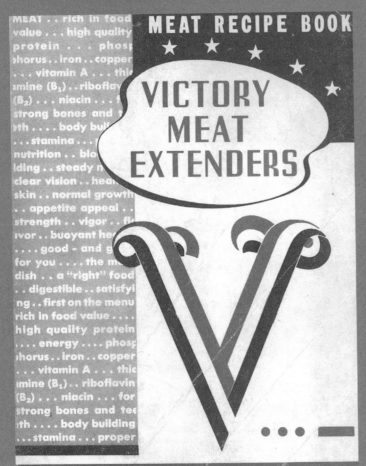

MEAT RECIPE BOOK

VICTORY MEAT EXTENDERS

V...

Compliments **NATIONAL LIVE STOCK AND MEAT BOARD**

Preserving Meat in Lard

"Use only fresh meat, and be sure that containers are sterile. To sterilize crock—turn crock upside down in a dishpan half full of water, and boil water for 15 minutes. Remove crock, but do not dry with cloth.

To pack meat in lard—cook meat as you would for serving. Place it in a dry sterilized crock and cover immediately with hot lard. Cover with clean waxpaper, then with crock cover or plate.

When removing meat from crock, be sure that remaining meat is well covered . . . Pour melted lard over it so that no air will touch it.

Small crocks are better than large ones, since the meat will not be disturbed as often."—*Food as We Like It*, 1943

Meat rationing did not go into effect until early in 1943 with the distribution of War Ration Book Two. Under the program, red ration stamps were needed to purchase fresh, frozen, cured, or canned beef, veal, pork, and lamb; all variety meats such as heart, liver, etc.; ready-to-serve meats like sausage and hot dogs; and canned meat, fish, and poultry. In addition, under the same program, butter, lard, margarine, shortening, salad and cooking oils, and cheese (except cottage) were rationed. Initially, each person was allotted 2½ pounds a week of the above foods requiring red ration stamps. That meant that the weight of any fats or cheese purchased was deducted from the ration budget for meat. Meat production in 1943 actually went up by almost 50 percent, but the shortages were explained by the increased demand for meat both at home and in the armed forces. The 25 percent increase in civilian meat purchases was attributed to increased worker incomes in the war industry, while increased military needs were due to the fact that servicemen's meat consumption was about two and a half times that of the average civilian.

When meat rationing began, Americans took a second look at the black market. Because of the cultural importance of meat in the American diet, it was the rationed commodity that people were most often willing to go to unpatriotic means to obtain. It was perceived that American men needed and deserved a certain amount of meat daily, and that in order to "do right by her man" the homemaker had to find a way to provide it. The government responded with posters and the Home Front Pledge to keep housewives and butchers honest, while food writers looked to Europe for enticing recipes using fresh game, poultry, and fish—which were not rationed—and the less desirable cuts of meat that carried fewer points. Point values were changed monthly depending upon the supplies available for the consumer market, and were posted in the store. Meat was hard to hoard, so the problem of providing it was a daily one. The shopper had to be constantly aware of the changing point values of different meats and of the number of points she had to work with.

When asked about meat, many home-front cooks remember inventing casseroles and one-pot meals that used meat for flavoring. They also remember saving their points for special occasions, and going to dinner parties where each couple would bring their own steak to cook and the host and hostess would provide the rest of the meal. My mother remembers joining with four friends to buy and raise a steer on a neighboring farm. It was cheaper than purchasing the meat from a butcher but you had the meat from a quarter of a steer all at one time. She said she canned most of the meat, but that she fried the steaks, layered them in crocks covered with lard, and stored them in the basement (American confit?). Other people described a similar technique. In this chapter you will find recipes for main dishes that provide varying amounts of protein. Included are unrationed chicken, fish, and game recipes, dishes using low-point stewing meats, variety meats, and sausages, and a few ways to recycle yesterday's roast into an entirely new dish.

ARROZ CON PATO

★ ★

International dishes were well received as special-occasion recipes. This one-pot meal is easy to prepare, full of flavor, and requires no ration stamps because duck was not rationed.

1 (5-pound) duck, cut into pieces
1 teaspoon vegetable shortening or
   bacon fat
1 cup coarsely chopped onions
2 cloves garlic

3 cups water
1 teaspoon curry powder
¾ teaspoon salt
¼ teaspoon ground black pepper
1¼ cups brown rice

Rinse duck and pat dry. Melt shortening in a 5-quart Dutch oven; brown duck pieces on all sides. Add onions and garlic; sauté until golden. Add ½ cup water, the curry powder, salt, and pepper. Bring to a boil; cover and simmer 45 minutes.

Remove fat from broth in Dutch oven; stir in remaining 2½ cups water and the rice. Cover and simmer 45 to 50 minutes longer or until duck and rice are tender. Serve from Dutch oven.

4 Servings

"One hundred pounds of meat roasted at 500°F. loses approximately 44 pounds, at 400° it loses 22 pounds, but at 300°F. only 12 pounds. Home Economists prefer flavor of meat roasted at low temperatures as well."—*American Cookery*, February 1944

STUFFED BEEF HEART

★ ★

There was new interest in variety meats because they were lower in both dollars and points than muscle meats and had very little waste. There will probably be leftovers from this roast to add to a soup or salad the next day.

2 tablespoons margarine or vegetable
   shortening
¼ cup chopped onion
¼ cup chopped celery
2 cups cubed day-old white bread
   (from 4 to 5 slices bread)

¼ cup finely chopped fresh parsley
¼ teaspoon salt
¼ teaspoon rubbed sage
⅛ teaspoon ground black pepper
1 (3- to 4-pound) beef heart

Melt margarine in a large skillet. Add onion and celery and sauté until lightly browned. Remove from heat and stir in bread cubes, parsley, salt, sage, and pepper. Set aside until cool enough to handle.

Preheat oven to 350°F. Remove and discard fat, veins, and arteries from heart; rinse and drain. Place on rack in roasting pan. Cut pocket in center.

When stuffing has cooled slightly, spoon into heart and skewer or sew top together. Add 1 inch water to pan, cover and roast until tender, 2½ to 3 hours.

To serve, remove skewers or stitches and slice crosswise.

6 Servings

BOILED TONGUE WITH HORSERADISH SAUCE

★ ★

This was a war economy meal that our family continued to enjoy well into the 1960s. The pressure cooker reduced the cooking time and the leftover broth and meat made both a delicious soup and pickled tongue for the next day.

1 (3½- to 4-pound) beef tongue
2 cups water
¾ teaspoon salt

½ cup sour cream
¼ cup grated fresh horseradish

Scrub the tongue under cool running water and drain; trim off root, gristle, and bones from cut end to make even. Place tongue in pressure cooker. Add water and ½ teaspoon salt; seal pan and heat to 15 pounds pressure following manufacturers' instructions. Cook 45 minutes.

Meanwhile, prepare Horseradish Sauce: Combine sour cream, horseradish, and ¼ teaspoon salt; spoon into serving bowl. Cover and refrigerate until ready to serve.

Remove pressure cooker from heat and place under cool running water until pressure subsides completely. Transfer tongue to bowl of cool water for 2 minutes; reserve cooking liquid. Pull off and discard skin; trim off any fat at large end. Reheat in cooking liquid if meat has cooled too much.

Thinly slice tongue and arrange on serving platter. Serve with Horseradish Sauce.

8 Servings

PORK-U-PINES

★ ★

Also made with just ground beef and called porcupine meatballs, these flavorful sausage balls become even more prickly when cooked in the pressure cooker.

¾ pound bulk pork sausage

¾ pound ground pork or beef

½ cup uncooked long-grain white rice

½ teaspoon salt

1 tablespoon vegetable shortening

1 cup water

¼ cup all-purpose flour

¼ teaspoon allspice

1½ cups milk

Preheat oven to 350°F.

Combine sausage, ground pork, rice, and ¼ teaspoon salt. Shape mixture into 18 meatballs.

Heat shortening in a 3-quart Dutch oven. Add meatballs and sauté until brown on all sides. Add water, cover, and roast 1 hour.

Remove meatballs to serving bowl; keep warm. Remove any fat from drippings in Dutch oven. Combine flour, allspice, and remaining ¼ teaspoon salt in a small bowl. Gradually beat in milk. Add milk mixture to drippings in Dutch oven and bring to a boil over medium heat, stirring constantly, until smooth. Spoon over meatballs and serve.

6 Servings

"Keep The Home Front Pledge
Pay no more than Ceiling Prices
Pay your Points in full"
—*Office of War Information Poster, 1942*

WARTIME SPECIAL

Emergency Steak

1 cup flaked wheat cereal

⅓ cup milk

2 tablespoons very finely
chopped onion

¾ teaspoon salt

¼ teaspoon ground black
pepper

1 pound ground beef

Combine cereal, milk, onion, salt, and pepper in a medium bowl; set aside 5 minutes.

Preheat broiler. Grease center of shallow roasting pan.

Stir ground beef into cereal mixture and place on the greased roasting pan. Pat into the shape of a T-bone steak.

Broil 6 inches from heat source until browned—about 5 minutes. Turn and broil on other side until cooked through—5 to 10 minutes longer.

Promoted by General Mills in both advertisements and recipe booklets, this whimsical wartime special would taste good no matter how you shaped it. I found it very difficult to turn when it was time to broil the second side until I used a small baking sheet as a large spatula.

6 Servings

PORK CHOP SUEY

★ ★

Also called American Chop Suey, this dish was as exotic as home-front cooking was likely to be. During the war, magazines ran articles about Chinese cooking, each reminding the reader that the Chinese were our friends and allies.

2 tablespoons vegetable oil

½ pound boned pork, cut into
    ½-inch pieces

1 cup thinly sliced celery

1 cup thinly sliced green bell peppers

1 cup sliced fresh mushrooms

1 cup thinly sliced onions

2 cups water

2 tablespoons soy sauce

2 tablespoons cornstarch

3 cups hot cooked rice

Canned fried noodles, optional

Heat oil in a 5-quart Dutch oven. Add pork and sauté over medium heat until lightly browned on all sides. Stir in celery, bell peppers, mushrooms, and onions; sauté, stirring constantly until vegetables are lightly browned.

Add 1¾ cups of the water and bring mixture to a boil over high heat. Reduce heat to medium and cook 15 minutes. Combine remaining ¼ cup water, the soy sauce, and cornstarch. Stir into pork mixture and cook, stirring constantly, until thickened.

Serve chop suey over rice. Top with fried noodles, if desired.

4 Servings

"When it comes to nutrition, the experts say that meat is meat—a fancy cut is no better for us than a thrifty one. It contains protein, minerals, and vitamins too valuable to lose. So never waste a morsel."—*Recipes for Today*, 1943

CORN BELT SPAGHETTI

★ ★

In the early 1940s, Americans were just learning to eat spaghetti, and most sauce recipes included ground beef. The use of the more easily available pork in this recipe probably gave them a more authentic sauce than usual. However, the All-American name cloaks the possibility that they might be learning to make "enemy food."

1 tablespoon finely chopped salt pork
  or vegetable shortening
1¼ pounds boneless pork shoulder,
  cut into 1-inch pieces
1 cup chopped onions
3 cloves garlic, finely chopped
1 quart home-canned tomatoes

1 (8-ounce) can tomato sauce
½ pound fresh mushrooms, sliced
¼ to ½ teaspoon red pepper flakes
¼ to ½ teaspoon salt
¼ teaspoon ground black pepper
1 (8-ounce) package spaghetti

Cook salt pork or melt shortening over medium heat in a heavy 3-quart saucepan. Add pork and sauté until browned on all sides, about 10 minutes. Add onions and garlic and cook, stirring occasionally, about 5 minutes longer.

Add tomatoes and tomato sauce; simmer until pork is very soft, 1 to 1½ hours, adding water occasionally, if necessary. Add mushrooms, pepper flakes to taste, ¼ to ½ teaspoon salt, and the ground pepper; cook 20 minutes longer.

Meanwhile, cook spaghetti in salted water according to package directions. Drain well and divide onto 4 plates. Top with sauce and serve.

4 Servings

RABBIT SAUTÉ

★ ★

Many families had wild rabbit during the war if there was someone who had time to go hunting. Wild rabbit can be used in this recipe, but you must cook it 20 to 30 minutes longer.

1 (2-pound) dressed rabbit, cut into
   8 pieces
3 tablespoons vegetable oil
¼ cup plus 2 tablespoons unsifted
   all-purpose flour
1 teaspoon curry powder
½ teaspoon salt

⅛ teaspoon ground black pepper
1½ cups water
1 cup milk
1 teaspoon Worcestershire sauce
2 tablespoons sherry, optional
1 tablespoon chopped fresh parsley

Rinse rabbit well and pat dry. Rub pieces with 1 tablespoon of oil. Combine ¼ cup flour, the curry powder, salt, and pepper in a pie plate. Dip rabbit into flour mixture to coat all over. Save any remaining flour mixture.

Heat 1 tablespoon oil in a 5-quart Dutch oven over medium heat; sauté rabbit pieces until well browned. Turn; add remaining tablespoon oil and sauté until browned on other side.

Add water, cover, and simmer 45 to 50 minutes or until tender.

Remove rabbit to serving platter. Stir remaining 2 tablespoons flour and any flour mixture saved from coating rabbit into milk. Skim fat from drippings in pan. Add milk mixture and Worcestershire sauce; cook, stirring constantly until thickened. Stir in sherry, if desired. Spoon some sauce over rabbit and pour rest into a gravy boat. Sprinkle rabbit with parsley and serve.

4 Servings

SPRING LAMB STEW

★ ★

Each red rationing stamp was printed with a letter indicating the week when the stamp could be used and a number which represented the number of points it was worth. Each week the number of points that the shopper had to give up for a rationed item was adjusted according to the availability of the item and in the case of meat in accordance with the amount of edible meat in a pound of that particular cut. Lamb shoulder tends to have considerable fat and bone and so was lower in points than the same weight of leg of lamb, for example.

1 tablespoon vegetable shortening or butter (or a mixture)	1/4 teaspoon ground black pepper
1 1/2 pounds lamb shoulder chops, cut into 1-inch pieces	4 medium carrots
	1 pound asparagus
2 cups water	1 bunch green onions
	1/2 cup milk
1/2 teaspoon salt	1/4 cup unsifted all-purpose flour

Melt shortening in a 4-quart Dutch oven; sauté lamb pieces until brown on all sides. Add water, salt, and pepper; bring to a boil. Cover and simmer until tender, 1 to 1 1/4 hours.

Meanwhile, peel and thinly slice carrots. Trim asparagus and green onions; cut diagonally into 2-inch pieces. When lamb is tender, add carrots, asparagus, and green onions. Cook until vegetables are just tender, about 6 to 8 minutes longer.

Remove lamb and vegetables to large casserole using a slotted spoon; discard any bones and pieces of fat. Stir together milk and flour until smooth. Remove fat from broth in Dutch oven; stir in milk mixture and cook, stirring constantly until gravy has thickened. Pour gravy over lamb and vegetables and serve.

6 Servings

SHEPHERD'S PIE

★ ★

Shepherd's Pie is usually made with lamb, but this thrifty version can be made with a measured amount of any cooked meat, or a mixture of several. I often make it with turkey leftovers the day after Thanksgiving.

1 teaspoon vegetable oil or
   shortening
½ cup coarsely chopped onion
2 cups homemade or canned meat or
   poultry broth
¼ cup unsifted all-purpose flour
⅛ teaspoon ground black pepper

3 cups cubed cooked lamb, beef,
   pork, or poultry
2 cups cooked leftover vegetables or
   1 (10-ounce) package frozen mixed
   vegetables
¼ teaspoon salt, optional
3 cups mashed potatoes
2 tablespoons grated Cheddar cheese

Preheat oven to 400°F. Heat oil in a medium skillet with ovenproof handle. Add onion and sauté just until it begins to brown. Add 1½ cups broth; bring to a boil over high heat.

Meanwhile, combine remaining ½ cup broth, the flour, and pepper. Stir into boiling broth and cook, stirring, until thickened. Stir in meat and vegetables; return to a boil. Taste and add salt, if needed.

Carefully spoon mashed potatoes over meat mixture and sprinkle with cheese. Bake until surface of mashed potatoes begins to brown, about 12 minutes. Serve from skillet.

4 Servings

"Help your dealer by shopping at hours when he is least busy; shopping in person; and asking no favors. Do as much of your week's shopping at one time as possible."—69 *Ration Recipes for Meat*, undated

MEAT ROLY POLY

★ ★

Wartime recipe collections were full of rolled dishes called roly polys. Sometimes they were main dishes and sometimes desserts, but they were all attractive ways of extending rationed or scarce foods with the addition of a less expensive cereal or egg product (such as the bread stuffing used here), biscuit dough, rice, or a soufflé layer.

½ pound ground beef

½ pound ground pork

½ pound ground veal

1 large egg

¾ teaspoon salt

¼ teaspoon ground black pepper

3 cups cubed day-old white bread
   (from 5 to 6 slices bread)

½ cup finely chopped onion

½ cup finely chopped red bell pepper

¼ cup milk

¼ cup finely chopped parsley

½ teaspoon dried marjoram leaves

1 tablespoon melted bacon fat or
   shortening

Preheat oven to 350°F. Grease a shallow roasting pan.

Combine beef, pork, veal, egg, ½ teaspoon salt, and the pepper in a medium bowl. Pat out to a 12-inch square on wax paper.

Combine bread cubes, onion, bell pepper, milk, parsley, marjoram, remaining ¼ teaspoon salt, and the bacon fat in same bowl. Pat in an even layer over meat. Roll up like a jelly roll on the wax paper and using ends of paper, lift roly poly into greased pan. Pull wax paper out from under roll.

Bake, uncovered, 45 to 50 minutes or until the center of roly poly feels firm when gently pressed.

To serve, cut roly poly crosswise into 8 slices.

8 Servings

WARTIME SPECIAL

Pig's Knuckles

4 pig's knuckles

8 cups water

1 teaspoon salt

½ cup chopped celery tops

2 cloves garlic

1 bay leaf

¼ teaspoon pepper

1 small head cabbage,
  quartered

Wash pig's knuckles and combine them with all other ingredients except cabbage in a large pot. Bring to a boil. Cover and simmer 2 hours or until tender. Add cabbage and cook 10 minutes longer. Remove and discard bay leaf before serving.

4 Servings

"I was a young girl, 18 years old, who was called on to fulfill the wish of some seamen whose ship had been bombed. They had gotten to New York bay and wished for a spaghetti and meatball dinner. I had to take a tug boat to get there. Cooking this meal in a huge galley with huge pots and a slab of frozen meat was not what I had expected but I managed the meal nevertheless."—*Concetta Loughlin, Staten Island, New York*

BAKED MEAT LOAF POTATOES

★ ★

The flavor of the beef filling permeates these baked potatoes, making a big meal from a little bit of ground meat.

4 large baking potatoes, scrubbed
½ pound ground beef
¼ cup finely chopped green bell pepper
¼ cup finely chopped celery
¼ cup finely chopped onion
½ teaspoon salt

⅛ teaspoon ground black pepper
2 tablespoons vegetable shortening or oil
3 tablespoons all-purpose flour
1¼ cups milk
2 tablespoons chopped celery leaves or parsley

Preheat oven to 400°F. Hollow out potatoes to make a boat. Finely chop the potato that was removed.

Combine chopped potato, ground beef, bell pepper, celery, onion, ¼ teaspoon salt, and the black pepper. Spoon mixture into hollows in potatoes, mounding on top.

Place potatoes in a baking pan and bake for 60 to 75 minutes or until they are tender.

Meanwhile, melt shortening or heat oil over medium heat; stir in flour and remaining ¼ teaspoon salt until smooth. Gradually stir in milk and cook, stirring constantly until thickened and boiling. Stir in celery leaves or parsley and keep warm until potatoes are tender. Serve sauce over potatoes.

4 Servings

"War or no war, the trout cries aloud for a sharp Rhine or Moselle wine; although you could plan something of a surprise by serving a nice cold bottle of Tavel (the best French Rosé from the Rhone)."—*Dining for Moderns,* 1940

BEEF VEGETABLE BURGERS

★ ★

The addition of vegetables to these burgers gives them a lot more flavor than the usual "just-meat" variety.

¾ pound ground beef
1 cup grated potato
½ cup grated carrot
¼ cup finely chopped onion
¼ cup finely chopped red or green
 bell pepper
1 large egg, lightly beaten

2 tablespoons ketchup
1 teaspoon chili powder
½ teaspoon salt
¼ teaspoon ground black pepper
2 teaspoons vegetable shortening or
 butter (or a mixture)
6 sandwich buns, optional

Combine beef, potato, carrot, onion, bell pepper, egg, ketchup, chili powder, salt, and black pepper in a medium bowl. Shape into 6 burgers.

Heat 1 teaspoon shortening over medium heat in a large heavy skillet. Add burgers and cook 10 minutes. Add remaining shortening; turn and cook until both meat and potato are cooked.

Serve on sandwich buns, if desired.

6 Servings

"My Grandparents raised turkeys and I helped kill turkeys and dress and process them in half gallon jars. An Aunt and Uncle had several hives of honey bees. We made dried apples and peaches. Others had 'sugar cane patches' and took it to the syrup mill."—*Meda Jane Trice, Sherman, Texas*

STUFFED PEPPERS

★ ★

This recipe can be adapted to meet the needs of any time period. Here, a very little bit of ground beef flavors a savory rice and vegetable filling.

4 medium bell peppers, either red or green

1 tablespoon vegetable shortening or butter (or a mixture)

¼ pound ground beef

½ cup chopped onion

½ cup long-grain white rice

1 cup water

½ cup fresh or frozen green peas

¼ cup grated carrot

½ teaspoon dried basil leaves

¼ to ½ teaspoon salt

¼ teaspoon ground black pepper

2 tablespoons grated Cheddar cheese

Bring 4 inches water to a boil in a large saucepan. Trim a 1-inch slice from top of each pepper. Discard stems; finely chop tops and set aside. Discard ribs and seeds from bottoms of peppers. Place peppers into boiling water; cook 5 minutes. Remove peppers to colander and drain upside down until filling is prepared.

Preheat oven to 375°F. Melt shortening in a large skillet over medium heat. Add ground beef, onion, and chopped pepper tops; sauté, stirring until beef has browned. Add rice, 1 cup water, fresh peas (if using frozen peas add them after rice is tender), carrot, basil, ¼ teaspoon salt and the black pepper. Bring mixture to a boil, reduce heat to low, and cook, covered, 15 to 18 minutes or until rice is tender and all liquid has been absorbed. Taste and add additional salt, if necessary.

Set peppers upright in a soufflé dish or deep baking pan. Divide filling among peppers; sprinkle with cheese. Bake 15 to 20 minutes or until cheese has melted.

4 Servings

MOTHER'S FRIED CHICKEN

★ ★

Although chicken wasn't rationed, we always thought of it as something special to serve on Sunday or for special celebrations. The trouble with a whole chicken is that when cut up there are some parts that no one really wants. My mother used to always insist that the backs, necks, and wings were her favorite parts and let my father and I have the legs, thighs, and breast pieces. I mentioned this recently to some friends and they remembered their mothers doing the same thing. It's possible there was a poster telling home-front mothers that the patriotic thing to do was to give the good parts to your family. Or perhaps it's just a part of being a mother.

1 (3½-pound) frying chicken, cut
   into 8 pieces
⅓ cup unsifted all-purpose flour
¼ teaspoon salt
⅛ teaspoon ground black
   pepper

1 large egg
⅓ cup unseasoned dry bread crumbs
2 tablespoons vegetable shortening or
   butter (or a mixture)
1½ cups water

Rinse and thoroughly drain chicken. Combine flour, salt, and pepper on a plate or in a plastic bag; add chicken pieces and turn or shake to coat completely; reserve any remaining flour. Lightly beat egg in a medium bowl; measure crumbs onto another plate. Dip flour-coated chicken pieces into egg and then into crumbs to coat completely.

Heat 1 tablespoon shortening over medium heat in 5-quart Dutch oven. Add as many chicken pieces as will fit and sauté until browned on all sides. When browned, remove chicken to one of the plates used above and brown remaining pieces, adding remaining shortening as necessary. Remove chicken pieces to plate.

Add a rack and 1 cup water to the Dutch oven in which you sautéed the chicken. Replace the chicken pieces. Bring water to a boil; cover, reduce heat to low, and simmer chicken until tender, about 45 minutes.

To serve, remove chicken to serving platter. Lift rack from Dutch oven. Skim off any fat from drippings. Beat remaining ½ cup water into the reserved flour mixture and stir into drippings in bottom of Dutch oven. Bring mixture to a boil over medium heat, stirring occasionally. Strain into a gravy boat and serve with fried chicken.

4 Servings

CURRIED CHICKEN FRICASSEE

★ ★

If you lived in the country and didn't raise chickens, the best way to buy a chicken was to go to the poultry farm and wait for them to kill and pluck one. I had no choice about going along on these excursions but at least I could hide away in the feed shed and avert my eyes by looking at the feed-bag fabric until after the chicken was ready for cooking. Once the chicken was purchased, I was allowed to select the fabric for my next outfit from the collection of printed feedbags the farmer's wife had neatly stacked into piles of stripes, flowers, and polka dots.

1 (4½- to 5-pound) stewing chicken,
    cut into 8 pieces

⅓ cup unsifted all-purpose flour

2 teaspoons curry powder

½ teaspoon salt

⅛ teaspoon ground black pepper

2 tablespoons vegetable shortening or
    butter (or a mixture)

2 cups water

¾ cup finely chopped onion

½ cup finely chopped carrot

½ cup finely chopped celery

Hot cooked long-grain white rice,
    optional

Rinse and thoroughly drain chicken. Combine flour, curry powder, salt, and pepper in a plastic bag; add chicken pieces and shake to coat completely.

Heat 1 tablespoon shortening over medium heat in a 5-quart Dutch oven. Add as many chicken pieces as will fit and sauté until browned on all sides. When browned, remove chicken to plate and brown remaining pieces, adding remaining shortening as necessary.

Return all chicken pieces to Dutch oven. Add water, onion, carrot, and celery. Bring water to a boil; cover, reduce heat to low, and simmer chicken until tender, about 1 to 1¼ hours.

To serve, remove chicken to serving bowl or casserole. Discard fat from broth in Dutch oven. Puree broth and vegetables in a food mill or food processor. Reheat, if necessary, and pour over chicken. Serve with rice, if desired.

4 Servings

CODFISH CASSEROLE

★ ★

Eggs extend the protein of the harder-to-come-by codfish in this nutritious casserole. Sometimes called Angel Codfish because of the light topping, this dish can be made with any mild-flavored white fish.

1 pound codfish fillet	⅛ teaspoon ground black pepper
2 tablespoons vegetable shortening or butter (or a mixture)	1¼ cups milk
	1 large egg, separated
2 tablespoons finely chopped green bell pepper	2 tablespoons pickle relish
	1 teaspoon Worcestershire sauce
2 tablespoons finely chopped onion	2 hard-cooked eggs, sliced
1 tablespoon all-purpose flour	¾ cup unseasoned dry bread crumbs
¼ teaspoon salt	1 tablespoon butter, melted

Preheat oven to 350°F. Generously grease a shallow 1-quart baking dish. Add codfish and bake 15 minutes.

Melt shortening over medium heat in heavy skillet. Add bell pepper and onion; sauté until golden. Stir in flour, salt, and black pepper until smooth. Very gradually stir in milk. Bring to a boil, stirring constantly until sauce has thickened. Remove from heat.

Meanwhile, beat egg white in a small bowl until soft peaks form. Beat egg yolk in another small bowl until thick. Gradually beat about one third of sauce into yolk. Return the mixture to the skillet of sauce along with pickle relish and Worcestershire sauce. Stir together; fold in beaten white.

Arrange hard-cooked eggs over fish in baking dish; top with sauce. Combine crumbs and butter; sprinkle over top. Place on rimmed baking sheet and bake 15 to 20 minutes longer.

6 Servings

SPANISH-STYLE BAKED FISH FILLETS

★ ★

A fisherman in the family was a real plus during the war; the use of fishing fleets for special wartime assignments meant that the commercial fish supply was light and sporadic. A flavorful extender, Spanish Sauce was a favorite addition to all kinds of meat, fish, and poultry.

2 tablespoons vegetable shortening or
    butter (or a mixture)

½ cup finely chopped onion

½ cup finely chopped green bell
    pepper

1 tablespoon all-purpose flour

1 teaspoon brown sugar

½ teaspoon dried marjoram leaves

¼ teaspoon salt

¼ teaspoon dried thyme leaves

⅛ teaspoon ground black pepper

1 pint home-canned or 1
    (15-ounce) can tomatoes

1 pound fish fillets (whatever you
    catch or can find in the market)

Preheat oven to 400°F. Generously grease a shallow 1-quart baking dish.

Melt shortening in heavy medium skillet over medium heat. Add onion and bell pepper; sauté until golden. Stir in flour, brown sugar, marjoram, salt, thyme, and black pepper until smooth. Very gradually stir in tomatoes. Bring to a boil, stirring constantly until sauce has thickened.

Arrange fish fillets in baking dish; top with sauce. Place on rimmed baking sheet and bake 12 to 15 minutes or until fish flakes easily.

4 Servings

> "Well over a million pounds of canned sea mussels were packed in the 1942–43 season. They were so well received, that a larger pack will be made next year."—*American Cookery*, November 1943

6

STRRRRRREEEEEEEETCH IT

★★★★★★★★★★★★★★★★★★★★

Adirondack Chowder	Five-Minute Steak Sandwiches
Chicken Bone Soup	Ham and Egg Pie
Hamburger Vegetable Soup	Homemade Scrapple
Navy Bean Soup	Baked Eggs in Cheese Sauce
Baked Beans with Bacon	Cabbage Delmonico
Baked Beans with Salt Pork and Molasses	Eggs in Noodle Nests
California "Chicken"	English Monkey
Fish Hash	Macaroni Goldenrod
Chicken and Waffles	Sauerkraut Croquettes

Despite rationing, there were many times when meat was hard to come by. Cooks were always aware that they had to make the little they could find go a long way. Creative uses of leftovers, meatless main dishes, small amounts of thinly sliced meat or ground meat to flavor a dish, and big pots of soup on the back burner became the expected fare for weekday meals. "Stretch" and "extend" entered the cook's everyday vocabulary.

Recipes devised during the Depression, when there was no money to buy meat, came back into fashion with a patriotic guise; carbohydrates such as potatoes, rice, noodles, and breads moved to the center of the plate as rings to be filled, mounds to be topped, or baked goods to hold meat, poultry, or fish-based sauces. Lists of "Uses for Leftovers" included everything from asparagus and roast beef to deviled eggs and prunes. In order to fit the needs of the day, a recipe had to be economical, convenient, and use few rationed foods. Ground beef became a star because it required fewer ration stamps per pound than roasts and chops, and because it could be divided into small portions to provide a little meat flavor for several meals.

While cheese is always an excellent alternate source of protein, most cheeses were rationed at the same time as meat. Less cheese was being made as more milk was shipped overseas in either liquid or dehydrated form and cheese was a convenient commodity to ship to Europe as well. But a little bit of cheese (by weight) goes a long way compared to the same weight of meat, so recipes used cheese in addition to eggs or bits of leftover meat to fill the protein requirement for a main dish. Casseroles found their place on the wartime menu because they are flexible, easy-to-make, and satisfying. In many articles, homemakers weren't even given recipes for casseroles, just guidelines for combining flavors. In the 1943 book *Cook It in a Casserole*, the author suggests that American cooks were following the lead of European cooks, who had been making casseroles for years. She credits the phenomenon to the fact that since ration points have "become as important as dollars," using leftovers was essential. Whether it was casseroles, soups, or meat-stretching vegetable dishes, frugal cooks were proud of their inventiveness. But their reputations were on the line and the meals had to taste good as well as be filling and nutritious.

My mother is still a champion at frugal cooking. I have always been impressed by the thrifty way in which she runs her kitchen. But I think I have now discovered some of her sources of information. I was amazed to find in the food pages of wartime magazines recipes for things that I had thought only she knew how to make. This chapter dishes up a selection of main dishes using small amounts of meat or other high-protein alternatives in ways you too will probably remember.

ADIRONDACK CHOWDER

★ ★

A supply of home-canned corn extends the season for this hearty fresh sweet corn chowder. If you can't find the soda crackers, use saltines. Don't try to split them, just spoon the whipped cream on top.

¼ pound salt pork or bacon, finely
   chopped

2 cups chopped onions

1 cup chopped green bell peppers

2 tablespoons all-purpose flour

6 cups milk

½ to 1 teaspoon salt

½ teaspoon ground black pepper

4 cups fresh sweet corn kernels or 1
   quart home-canned sweet corn
   boiled 15 minutes and drained

6 soda crackers, split

¼ cup heavy cream, whipped

Heat salt pork in a 5-quart Dutch oven or soup pot over medium heat until it releases some fat. Add onions and bell peppers and sauté until pork and vegetables start to brown. Stir in flour until smooth. Gradually add milk, ½ teaspoon salt, and the black pepper. Bring to a boil, stirring constantly until thickened. Stir in corn; cook 5 minutes. Taste and add more salt, if necessary.

To serve, divide chowder into 6 soup plates or bowls. Fill split crackers with cream and float 1 on each bowl of chowder.

6 Servings

"Thick, nourishing soups are patriotic 'extenders,' perfect to ladle out of an old-fashioned tureen at the family table."—*Recipes for Today*, 1943

CHICKEN BONE SOUP

★ ★

This recipe works just as well with the bones from your holiday turkey. I usually divide them into 2 packages and freeze them so we can have two pots of soup to remember the holiday by. I make and freeze broth from the bones of every roast that I cook. You never know when you will want it for soup or sauce.

Bones and any meat scraps from 1
   (6-pound) roasting chicken
8 cups water
1 teaspoon butter
½ cup chopped onion
2 cloves garlic, finely chopped
1 cup chopped potato
½ cup sliced carrot

½ cup sliced celery
½ to 1 teaspoon salt
½ teaspoon dried basil leaves
¼ teaspoon dried thyme leaves
¼ teaspoon ground black pepper
½ cup fresh or frozen sweet corn
   kernels
½ cup frozen green peas

Bring bones and water to a boil in a 5-quart Dutch oven or soup pot over high heat. Reduce heat to low, cover, and simmer 1 hour. With tongs remove as many bones as possible to a large colander placed over a large bowl. Pour broth through colander into bowl. Rinse and dry Dutch oven.

Melt butter in Dutch oven. Add onion and garlic and sauté over medium heat until they start to brown. Remove colander of bones to a baking pan. Add broth, potato, carrot, celery, ½ teaspoon salt, the basil, thyme, and pepper to Dutch oven. Bring soup to a boil over high heat, reduce heat to low, and simmer 15 minutes.

Meanwhile, remove any chicken remaining on bones in colander. When soup has simmered 15 minutes, add chicken, corn, and peas; return to a boil and cook 5 minutes longer or until vegetables are tender. Taste and add additional salt, if necessary.

4 to 6 Servings

HAMBURGER VEGETABLE SOUP

Once we had a freezer, my mother would deglaze the skillet after cooking hamburgers and freeze the broth it made. She would gradually collect enough to make a flavorful soup using this same recipe only without the ground chuck. Don't worry; we always had sandwiches or cheese and crackers with it to provide the protein.

½ pound ground chuck

1 cup chopped onions

1 cup chopped green bell peppers

6 cups water

1 cup chopped carrots

1 cup chopped celery

1 cup chopped mushrooms

1 cup yellow corn kernels

1 cup fresh or frozen green peas

½ to 1 teaspoon salt

½ teaspoon ground black pepper

Cook ground chuck in 5-quart Dutch oven or heavy soup pot over medium heat, stirring occasionally until browned. Add onions and bell peppers and sauté until vegetables start to brown.

Stir in water, carrots, celery, mushrooms, corn, and peas. Bring to a boil, stirring constantly; cook 10 minutes or until vegetables are tender. Add salt to taste and the black pepper. Transfer to soup tureen and serve.

4 to 6 Servings

"Points saved are points earned. Make the most of unrationed foods and your backlog of points will always be ample."—*Ladies' Home Journal*, October 1943

NAVY BEAN SOUP

★ ★

In this soup, the beans extend the pound of meat to make 8 servings. This is a good meal to have simmering on the back burner when you don't know exactly when the family will get home for dinner. It is also something that can be made after dinner and refrigerated so that older children or even Dad can reheat it if Mom is working late.

2 cups navy beans	½ to 1 teaspoon salt
1 teaspoon vegetable shortening or butter (or a mixture)	½ teaspoon ground black pepper
1 pound beef brisket	2 cups chopped fresh tomatoes or 1 (15-ounce) can diced tomatoes
2 cups chopped onions	¼ cup thinly sliced celery
8 cups water	1 tablespoon chopped celery leaves

Pick through beans and discard any discolored ones or foreign material. Rinse beans thoroughly and bring to a boil with water to cover in a 3-quart saucepan. Cover, remove from heat, and set aside 1 hour. Drain and rinse beans.

Heat shortening in 5-quart Dutch oven or soup pot over medium heat. Add beef and brown on both sides. Add onions and sauté until they start to brown. Add water, beans, ½ teaspoon salt, and the pepper. Bring to a boil; cover and simmer until beans are very tender, 50 to 60 minutes.

Remove beef to a cutting board and cut into ½-inch cubes. Return beef to soup along with the tomatoes and celery. Bring to a boil and cook, stirring 10 minutes or until celery is tender. Taste and add additional salt, if necessary. Top with celery leaves and serve.

8 Servings

WARTIME SPECIAL

Baked Frankfurters with Stuffing

4 frankfurters
1 cup bread cubes
2 tablespoons finely chopped
   onion

2 tablespoons butter, melted
1 tablespoon chopped fresh
   parsley

Split frankfurters lengthwise. Combine bread, onion, butter, and parsley. Divide into frankfurters. Bake in 375°F. oven for 30 minutes.

"I and another lady walked our children to school each day. As we were nearing the local store, she said, 'what are you having for dinner?' 'Stuffed green peppers,' was my answer. 'Where the **** did you get the meat?' she said. 'Couple of cans of Spam,' said I. (Spam was not rationed and we could get it all the time because most men did not want to eat it. However, we liked it.) When she recovered, she said, 'What do you do with it?' 'Put it through the grinder, add eggs, rolled oats and rice, some herbs and go on as though it was ground meat,' was my reply. She stopped at the grocery store and had stuffed green peppers for dinner and her husband ate it."—*Melva Truka, Imperial, Missouri*

BAKED BEANS WITH BACON

★ ★

High in nutrition and easy to make, baked beans met all the needs for a wartime favorite. Our family is divided by baked bean recipes. One side favors salty and the other sweet. This simple recipe comes from my father's family. It was a favorite during the war and has since starred at five decades of family reunions.

1 pound Great Northern or other
    white beans
6 cups water
1 ham bone, optional (but great if
    you have one)

½ to ¾ teaspoon salt
¼ teaspoon ground red pepper
    (cayenne)
6 slices bacon, halved

Pick through beans and discard any discolored ones or foreign material. Rinse beans thoroughly and bring to a boil with water to cover in a 5-quart saucepan. Cover, remove from heat, and set aside 1 hour.

Drain, rinse, and return beans to saucepan with water, ham bone, if using, ½ teaspoon salt with ham bone or ¾ teaspoon without, and red pepper. Bring to a boil, cover and simmer 45 to 60 minutes or until tender.

Heat oven to 350°F. Remove ham bone; trim off and coarsely chop any meat from the bone. Stir meat into beans. Transfer beans to a 2-quart baking dish. Top with bacon and bake, uncovered, 30 to 35 minutes or until bacon has browned. Serve from baking dish.

8 Servings

BAKED BEANS WITH SALT PORK AND MOLASSES

★ ★

My mother's family always makes this type of sweet molasses-flavored baked beans. It was a perfect dish for the war years because it could be made in a covered casserole and kept warm in a 300°F oven for a while, if someone in the family had to work extra late.

1 pound navy or pea beans
½ pound salt pork
1 large onion, coarsely chopped
6 cups water
2 teaspoons dry mustard
½ teaspoon salt

½ teaspoon ground red pepper
  (cayenne)
½ cup light molasses
¼ cup packed light brown sugar
¼ cup ketchup

Pick through beans and discard any discolored ones or foreign material. Rinse beans thoroughly and bring to a boil with water to cover in a 5-quart saucepan. Cover, remove from heat, and set aside 1 hour.

Drain and rinse beans; dry saucepan. Sauté salt pork and onion in saucepan over medium heat until they begin to brown. Return beans to saucepan with water, mustard, salt, and red pepper. Bring to a boil, cover, and simmer 45 to 60 minutes or until tender.

Heat oven to 350°F. Stir molasses, brown sugar, and ketchup into beans. Transfer beans to a 2-quart casserole with lid. Bake 30 to 35 minutes or until top has formed a crust. Serve from casserole or hold in 300°F oven until ready to serve, up to 2 hours. If holding in oven, check periodically for dryness and add water if necessary.

8 Servings

CALIFORNIA "CHICKEN"

★ ★

By 1943, canned tuna was hard to buy because the tuna fleets had gone to war. Nonetheless, producers never stopped telling homemakers in their magazine advertisements that they would soon be able to serve their families recipes like this one. Actually, this dish would be equally good with any cooked fish leftovers.

1 cup chopped potatoes	3 tablespoons all-purpose flour
1 cup chopped carrots	½ teaspoon salt
1 cup fresh or drained canned green peas	¼ teaspoon ground black pepper
	1½ cups milk
1 tablespoon vegetable shortening	1 (6-ounce) can tuna packed in oil
1 medium onion, finely chopped	¼ cup unflavored bread crumbs

Combine potatoes, carrots, fresh peas (if using canned peas, add at end of cooking time), and water to cover in a 2-quart saucepan. Bring to a boil over high heat; cook just until vegetables are tender, about 10 minutes.

Preheat oven to 400°F. Grease a 1½- to 2-quart casserole.

Drain vegetables, reserving ½ cup cooking liquid. In same saucepan, melt shortening over medium heat and sauté onion until golden. Stir in flour, salt, and pepper until onion is evenly coated. Gradually stir in milk and reserved cooking liquid. Bring to a boil over medium heat, stirring constantly until white sauce has thickened.

Drain tuna, reserving 1 tablespoon oil. Break the tuna into flakes. Layer half of vegetables, half of white sauce, the tuna, remaining vegetables, and remaining white sauce in the greased casserole. Combine crumbs and 1 tablespoon reserved oil and sprinkle over top.

Bake until crumbs have browned and mixture bubbles, 20 to 25 minutes. Serve from casserole.

4 Servings

FISH HASH

★ ★

America's fresh-water lakes and streams were a favorite, free, and unregulated source of fresh fish. This hash was a quick way to dress up the leftovers for the next day's dinner.

2 slices bacon, cut into 1-inch pieces

1 cup coarsely chopped onions

2 cups flaked cooked fish

2 cups chopped cooked potatoes

¼ cup water

1 tablespoon grated horseradish

1 tablespoon prepared mustard

¼ teaspoon salt

⅛ teaspoon ground black pepper

Fry bacon in a large heavy skillet until pieces are crisp. Remove pieces to a small bowl.

Add onions to bacon fat in skillet and sauté until golden. Add fish, potatoes, water, horseradish, mustard, salt, and pepper to onion mixture. Cover and cook until hot through, 10 to 15 minutes.

To serve, sprinkle reserved bacon over top. Divide mixture in skillet into quarters; remove to serving plates using 2 spatulas.

4 Servings

Equal to a Serving of Meat as a Source of Protein:

"A serving of fish, shellfish, poultry, game, or a variety meat such as liver, kidney, heart, etc.; two medium eggs, one pint milk, about 6 tablespoons cottage cheese, about 2 ounces American cheese, 4 tablespoons peanut butter, about ¾ cup cooked soybeans, ¾ to 1 cup other beans, 1 cup cereal main dish such macaroni and cheese."—*Good Housekeeping*, September 1943

CHICKEN AND WAFFLES

★ ★

Waffle-making was an event in our house. We always baked them right at the table and everyone got a section of each waffle, hot from the iron.

Waffles:

1¾ cups unsifted all-purpose flour

4 teaspoons baking powder

¼ teaspoon salt

1½ cups milk

2 large eggs, separated

1 tablespoon melted butter

3 tablespoons shortening

Chicken Gravy:

2½ cups chicken broth

⅓ cup unsifted all-purpose flour

¼ to ½ teaspoon salt

¼ teaspoon ground black pepper

2 cups cut-up leftover cooked chicken (cut into 1-inch pieces)

2 tablespoons finely chopped pimiento, optional

1 tablespoon finely chopped fresh parsley

Preheat oven to 200°F. Place an ungreased baking sheet in the oven. Preheat waffle iron.

Prepare waffles: Combine flour, baking powder, and salt in a medium bowl. Beat together milk, egg yolks, and butter in a small bowl. Beat egg whites with an electric beater until stiff peaks form.

Make a well in center of flour mixture. Add milk mixture and stir just until all dry ingredients have been moistened. Do not overbeat. Fold in beaten whites.

Brush waffle iron with shortening and bake waffles following manufacturer's directions. Remove waffles to oven to keep warm until all have been baked.

Prepare chicken gravy: Gradually beat broth into ⅓ cup flour in a heavy 2-quart saucepan. Add ¼ teaspoon salt and the pepper; bring mixture to a boil over medium heat, stirring frequently until thickened. Taste and add more salt, if necessary. Stir in chicken, pimiento, if using, and parsley. Keep warm until all waffles have been baked.

To serve, cut waffles into sections; divide onto 6 plates. Top with chicken mixture and serve immediately.

6 Servings

FIVE-MINUTE STEAK SANDWICHES

★ ★

This recipe appears in many wartime magazines and cookbooks under a variety of names. It is not only quick and easy but makes a ½-pound of ground beef go a long way.

¼ cup old-fashioned rolled oats

¼ cup milk

4 slices firm white bread

2 teaspoons softened butter

2 teaspoons prepared mustard

½ pound ground chuck

2 tablespoons finely chopped onion

2 tablespoons finely chopped green
 bell pepper

¼ teaspoon salt

¼ teaspoon ground black pepper

Preheat broiler. Combine rolled oats and milk; set aside. Arrange bread on broiler pan; spread with half of butter and broil, watching carefully, until just golden. Remove pan from broiler.

Turn bread slices over; spread with remaining butter and mustard. Stir ground chuck, onion, bell pepper, salt, and black pepper into oats mixture. Spread onto bread slices in an even layer that reaches all the way to the crusts.

Broil sandwiches, 5 inches from heat source, 5 minutes or until meat is cooked through.

4 Servings

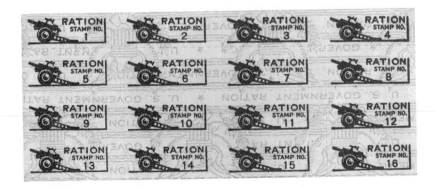

HAM AND EGG PIE

★ ★

A little bit of ham gives flavor to this pie, while the unrationed eggs extend the protein the dish provides. I have seen this called Easter Egg Pie, and it certainly is the perfect way to use the leftovers from Easter. It also makes a delicious main dish for brunch.

¼ cup vegetable shortening or butter (or a mixture)	½ teaspoon salt
½ cup coarsely chopped onion	⅛ teaspoon ground black pepper
½ cup coarsely chopped celery	3 hard-cooked large eggs, peeled and quartered lengthwise
¼ cup chopped green bell pepper	1 cup coarsely chopped ham
1¼ cups unsifted all-purpose flour	2 teaspoons baking powder
2⅓ cups milk	3 tablespoons grated Cheddar cheese

Preheat oven to 375°F. Grease a shallow 1-quart casserole or baking dish. Melt 1 tablespoon shortening in a large skillet over medium heat. Add onion, celery, and bell pepper; sauté until lightly browned.

Stir ¼ cup flour into vegetables until they are evenly coated. Stir in 2 cups milk, ¼ teaspoon salt, and the black pepper. Bring to a boil, stirring constantly until thickened.

Pour half of vegetable sauce into greased casserole. Arrange eggs in sauce. Sprinkle ham pieces around eggs; top with remaining sauce.

Combine remaining 1 cup flour, the baking powder, and remaining ¼ teaspoon salt. Cut remaining 3 tablespoons shortening into flour mixture with a pastry blender. Add remaining ⅓ cup milk and stir together. Pat out dough on wax paper to size of top of casserole. Slide onto ham and egg mixture and sprinkle with cheese. Bake pie 20 to 25 minutes or until topping is well browned.

4 Servings

WARTIME SPECIAL

Meat Fritters

¾ cup flour
1 teaspoon baking powder
¼ teaspoon salt
1 egg

¼ cup milk
1 tablespoon melted lard
1 pound leftover meat, thinly
  sliced

Heat lard or oil to 365°F. In a small bowl, stir together flour, baking powder, and salt; beat in egg, milk, and lard to make a batter. Dip pieces of meat in batter and fry until nicely browned.

"I best remember the ration meat stamps going for our new baby's canned milk supply while we ate pinto beans with a sprinkle of cheese. He was worth it!"—*Winifred M. Strom, Prescott, Arizona*

HOMEMADE SCRAPPLE

★ ★

Although pork was rationed, supplies remained good and it was frequently the meat that was easiest to find and lowest in points. Scrapple is by its nature a thrifty meal and can be served any time of the day. The addition of a fried or scrambled egg to each serving would help meet the day's protein requirement.

½ pound boneless pork shoulder, cut
   into 1-inch pieces
1 cup white cornmeal
2 tablespoons chopped celery leaves
2 tablespoons chopped fresh parsley
1 teaspoon salt
¼ teaspoon allspice

¼ teaspoon ground black pepper
¼ teaspoon rubbed sage
¼ cup unsifted all-purpose flour
Lard or vegetable shortening for
   frying
Golden syrup, light corn syrup, or
   honey, optional

Cook pork in water to cover in large heavy saucepan until tender, 35 to 40 minutes. Meanwhile, grease an 8-inch loaf pan.

Drain pork, reserving broth in a glass 1-quart measuring cup. If necessary, add water to broth to make 4 cups.

Grind (or process) pork and any fat attached to it. Return pork and broth to same saucepan. Gradually stir in cornmeal, celery leaves, parsley, salt, allspice, pepper, and sage. Bring to a boil over low heat, stirring constantly; cook 15 minutes continuing to stir.

Transfer scrapple mixture to prepared pan. Cool scrapple to room temperature, then cover and refrigerate several hours or overnight to cool completely.

To serve, unmold scrapple onto cutting board. Cut loaf crosswise into 12 slices. Dip both sides of slices in flour. Heat lard or shortening in a large skillet. Fry, several pieces at a time, until lightly browned on both sides, about 5 minutes. Keep warm until all scrapple has been fried; serve with syrup, if desired.

6 Servings

BAKED EGGS IN CHEESE SAUCE

★ ★

If cheese is in short supply, make the sauce without it and sprinkle a little over the top. Leftover green vegetables such as peas, sliced asparagus, or broccoli would make a good addition to the sauce if they are available.

2 tablespoons vegetable shortening or butter (or a mixture)	2 cups milk
¼ cup all-purpose flour	¾ cup grated Cheddar cheese
2 teaspoons dry mustard	6 large eggs
½ teaspoon salt	½ cup dry bread crumbs
	1 tablespoon melted butter

Preheat oven to 350°F. Grease a shallow 1-quart baking dish.

Melt shortening in a heavy 1-quart saucepan. Remove from heat. Stir in flour, mustard, and salt until smooth. Gradually stir in milk. Bring to a boil over low heat, stirring constantly until thick. Fold in cheese until completely melted.

Pour half of cheese sauce into greased baking dish. Make 6 indentations in sauce; break an egg into each. Spoon remaining sauce over eggs.

Combine bread crumbs and melted butter. Sprinkle over egg mixture. Bake until egg yolks are just firm, about 20 minutes. Serve immediately.

6 Servings

> "Good meat extenders which carry the flavor of meat and yet increase the number of servings include vegetables, gravies, sauces, noodles, spaghetti, macaroni, prepared cereals, oatmeal, cornmeal, bread crumbs, bread dressing, crackers, rice, dumplings, biscuits, bread or toast and others."—69 *Ration Recipes for Meat*, undated

CABBAGE DELMONICO

★ ★

This meatless main dish still reappears in fall vegetable articles and gardening cookbooks. The succulent wedges of cabbage need only a fraction of the cooking time often recommended in the 1940s.

1 (2-pound) head cabbage	½ teaspoon salt
2 tablespoons vegetable shortening or butter (or a mixture)	2 cups milk
	1 cup grated Cheddar cheese
3 tablespoons all-purpose flour	½ cup day-old white bread crumbs
½ teaspoon dry mustard	(from about 1⅓ slices bread)
¾ teaspoon paprika	1 teaspoon butter, melted

Preheat oven to 350°F. Generously grease a shallow 9-inch baking dish.

Cut cabbage into 6 wedges. Cook in boiling water to cover until crisp-tender, about 8 minutes; drain very well.

Meanwhile, melt shortening in a heavy saucepan, over low heat. Stir in flour, mustard, ½ teaspoon paprika, and the salt until smooth. Very gradually stir in milk; cook over low heat, stirring constantly until sauce has thickened. Fold in cheese.

Arrange drained cabbage in baking dish. Top with cheese sauce. Combine crumbs and butter. Sprinkle evenly over top. Sprinkle remaining ¼ teaspoon paprika over crumbs.

Place on rimmed baking sheet and bake 15 to 20 minutes or until browned.

6 Servings

"Bones, trimmings and meat drippings, once carelessly tossed aside, are now treasured for the fine flavor they extend to other foods."—*Victory Meat Extenders*, 1942

EGGS IN NOODLE NESTS

★ ★

Noodle and pasta main dishes were recommended as a way to provide a hearty meal while using few rationed foods. It would be hard to find an easier way to make dinner in a hurry.

2 cups ¼-inch-wide egg noodles

½ cup milk

¼ teaspoon salt

¼ teaspoon ground black pepper

½ cup grated Cheddar cheese

6 large eggs

Preheat oven to 350°F. Grease a shallow 1-quart baking dish.

Cook noodles according to package directions. Drain well and place in large bowl. Add milk, salt, and pepper. Transfer noodle mixture to greased baking dish. Sprinkle cheese over top.

Make 6 indentations in noodle mixture; break an egg into each. Bake until egg yolks are just firm, about 20 minutes. Serve immediately.

6 Servings

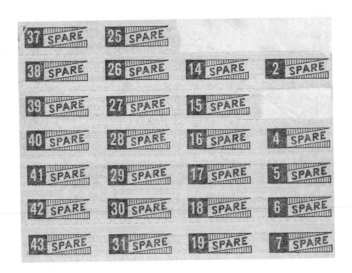

ENGLISH MONKEY

★ ★

This cheese-flavored bread sauce is somewhere between scrambled eggs and rarebit. The concept of extending inexpensive protein sources with bread harkens back to the Depression Era, but the milk, eggs, and cheese certainly make it a good source of nutrition—the sort of comforting dish you would like to have on a cold, stormy evening.

1¼ cups milk

1 cup fresh white bread crumbs

3 large eggs

1 tablespoon butter

1 tablespoon finely chopped onion

¾ cup grated cheese

½ teaspoon salt

⅛ teaspoon hot red pepper (cayenne)

4 slices warm toast

Combine milk and bread crumbs; set aside 5 minutes. Meanwhile, beat eggs until thick and light.

Melt butter in a heavy 2-quart saucepan. Add onion and sauté over medium heat until golden. Stir in crumb mixture, beaten eggs, cheese, salt, and cayenne. Cook, stirring constantly over low heat until mixture bubbles and cheese is uniformly melted. Place toast on serving plates; divide cheese mixture onto toast. Serve.

4 Servings

"Budgeting your meat Rations: Meat is a vital food, both for the nutrition of our armed forces and for our families on the home front. The body-building proteins supplied by meats are so high in nutritional quality that nutritionists recommend that at least 50% of the daily protein intake come from animal sources."—*69 Ration Recipes for Meat*, undated

MACARONI GOLDENROD

★ ★

Unrationed eggs star in this hearty dish. In postwar years, this sauce and topping appeared on toast as an alternate to creamed dried beef for lunch or supper. This definitely needs to be accompanied by a green vegetable.

1 (8-ounce) package macaroni	½ teaspoon salt
2½ cups milk	¼ teaspoon ground black pepper
⅓ cup unsifted all-purpose flour	6 hard-cooked large eggs, shelled

Cook macaroni according to package directions. Drain very well.

Meanwhile, in a heavy saucepan, beat milk into flour until smooth. Add salt and pepper. Cook over low heat, stirring constantly until sauce has thickened.

Coarsely chop egg whites and stir into sauce. Press egg yolks through a strainer. Transfer macaroni to a serving bowl. Spoon sauce over macaroni and top with egg yolk. Serve immediately.

4 to 6 Servings

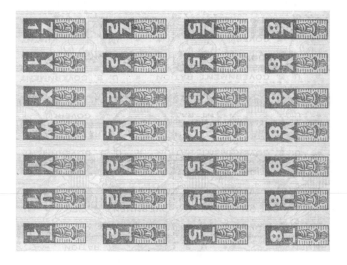

SAUERKRAUT CROQUETTES

★ ★

In the forties, croquettes were made from all sorts of leftover ingredients. Although this version is short on protein, it was promoted as a meatless main dish. The combination fascinated me and turned out to be so delicious that I now make it as an accompaniment to pork dishes.

1½ cups sauerkraut

1½ cups cooked long-grain white rice

1 large egg

¼ cup unsifted all-purpose flour

1 teaspoon baking powder

½ teaspoon salt

⅛ teaspoon ground black pepper

1 cup corn flakes, crushed

Vegetable oil for deep frying

Preheat deep fat to 375°F or oven to 400°F.

Combine sauerkraut, rice, egg, flour, baking powder, salt, and pepper. Divide mixture into 8 croquettes; coat in corn flake crumbs and deep fry 3 to 4 minutes, or until golden brown and center is hot. Or, place in oven and bake 15 to 20 minutes, until center is hot.

4 Servings

> "Save the liquor that remains when vegetables are cooked. It's rich in vitamins and minerals; adds flavor to sauces, gravies, vegetable cocktails. Keep it in a covered jar in your refrigerator. Save fruit juices and syrups for cold drinks, gelatin and other desserts."—*Frigidaire Advertisement, 1943*

7

BUTTER AND GUNPOWDER

★★★★★★★★★★★★★★★★★★★★★★

Buttermilk Dressing

Cooked Salad Dressing

Oil and Vinegar Dressings

Wartime French Dressing

Apricot Corn Bread

Low-Fat Muffins

Spoon Bread

Blueberry Cobbler

Brown Betty

Cherry Pudding

Applesauce Cake

Bread Crumb Cookies

Crumb Cake

Dutch Apple Cake

War Cake

Whipped Cream Cake

With the introduction of point rationing and War Ration Book Two in February of 1943, meat, butter, margarine, canned fish, cheese, canned milk, fats, and oils were rationed. Shortages of both meat and fats during the early winter had caused alarm in Washington. When the government estimated that the 1943 civilian butter supply would fall 15 percent below demand, and two additional sources of fat (coconut oil and palm oil from the Philippines and East Indies) were lost to the enemy, the decision was made. Citizens polled said that they preferred rationing to the inequalities that were expected to result as shortages increased.

This was the first rationing program in which shoppers were able to pick and choose among available items and decide which to "spend" their points for. The little red stamps became a kind of currency that required special government ration banks and a lot of extra work for grocers. Of the rationed fats, butter was the most missed and the most talked about. Shortening and vegetable oil were in greater supply, cost less, and required fewer ration points to buy. When you ask home-front cooks about fats during the war, they rarely mention margarine, shortening, and salad oil rationing. Butter deprivation and collecting scrap fats are the factors that they remember most.

People also remember the white margarine. Early in the history of margarine, butter manufacturers had managed to get laws passed in many states taxing the coloring of margarine so it was purchased white and had to be colored at home. In some states, food service establishments were prohibited from coloring margarine at all. I remember the large blocks of white margarine on the table at the summer camp I attended just after the war. We all chose to call it "cold cream."

Although fat from bacon and other meats could be and often was, substituted for butter as a cooking fat, the government recommended another use for them. Magazine articles and government posters counseled homemakers to save fats for making the glycerin used in explosives. Homemakers were told that a tablespoon of fat saved each day would make a pound a month. A pound from every home each month would make more than 500 million pounds of smokeless powder a year. Readers were directed to save the fat from deep-fat frying, meat drippings, and the rendered trimmings from steaks and chops; strain it and when a pound had been collected, take it to a butcher, who would pay the prevailing price for it in cash or ration stamps depending upon the program that was in effect at that time period.

Because butter was so sorely missed, what was available was saved for special occasions. To make it go farther, recipes recommended making spreads such as Honey Butter to use as a spread for bread and taught homemakers how to double the volume of butter by whipping it with an unflavored gelatin mixture or combining it with an equal amount of margarine. Well into the 1950s, my mother continued to whip together a pound of softened butter and a pound of margarine to make our table spread. Until I started this research, I never knew why. Lists of tips were everywhere to remind homemakers to thinly spread bread and rolls before serving (rather than putting a butter dish on the table), to use dried herbs, seasoned salts, and broth rather than butter on vegetables, and to use processed cheese, jelly, and peanut butter for spreads in place of butter. Do you know someone who opens only one end of a stick of butter and then rubs it over warm toast, corn on the cob, or on top of a bowl of vegetables? It might seem rude now, but that was perfectly acceptable, patriotic behavior in the summer of '43.

Most wartime cake recipes called for vegetable shortening. Where butter appeared in a recipe it was either for a very special occasion such as Christmas or a wedding, an old recipe that hadn't been changed (I found one where the editors called for shortening in the ingredient list but had forgotten to change the "butter" in the directions), or a tiny bit of butter was used in a crumb topping or over vegetables where it would be fully appreciated. In addition to replacing butter in baked goods, substituting for oil in salad dressings was an area in which homemakers needed help. Some of the recipes they used are included here. The baking recipes in this chapter often suggest that you substitute butter if you can get it—and today we can. So you can choose between using shortening for authenticity or butter for the flavor home-front cooks dreamed of.

BUTTERMILK DRESSING

★ ★

This tangy dressing uses no oil and makes excellent coleslaw or potato salad. These days when I get a quart of buttermilk, I freeze some of it in 1-cup portions so that it won't be pushed to the back of the refrigerator and spoil.

2 tablespoons prepared mustard

2 tablespoons cider vinegar

1 tablespoon light brown sugar

1 teaspoon salt

1 teaspoon paprika

⅛ teaspoon hot red pepper (cayenne)

1 cup buttermilk

Stir together the mustard, vinegar, brown sugar, salt, paprika, and red pepper in a pint jar with a tight-fitting lid.

Add the buttermilk; cover and shake until combined.

About 1 Cup

"This country has had to make the choice between 'guns and butter' in the sense that the weapons of war come before domestic comforts. But in our actual supply of butter itself we are lucky beyond all other nations at war. In 1942, the average consumption of butter was about 16 pounds. By reducing this consumption in 1943, we can continue to provide each soldier twice as much butter as the average civilian, and will help keep him in the physical condition to withstand the Iceland climate or keep a sure eye on a bombsight."—*Battle Stations for All*, 1943

COOKED SALAD DRESSING

This versatile dressing is low in oil and sugar, yet can be used in anything that you would normally dress with mayonnaise. I particularly like it for potato salad and sandwich fillings.

2 tablespoons all-purpose flour

2 tablespoons light brown sugar

2 teaspoons dry mustard

½ teaspoon salt

⅛ teaspoon hot red pepper (cayenne)

1 cup milk

3 tablespoons vegetable oil

⅓ cup cider vinegar or lemon juice

2 large eggs, lightly beaten

Combine flour, brown sugar, mustard, salt, and red pepper in the top of a double boiler. Gradually stir in milk and oil. Place over hot, not boiling, water; cook, stirring occasionally, until thickened.

Combine vinegar and eggs in a small bowl. Gradually stir egg mixture into milk mixture. Cook over hot water, stirring constantly until thickened. Pour into a jar and refrigerate until ready to use. Use within 3 or 4 days.

About 1½ Cups

"We had cows to milk by hand and I churned and 'worked' the butter in a large wooden bowl with a paddle of wood also. My fondest memories are of lowering the butter and whipping cream down into the open well in a bucket on a rope. What treasures we stored there!"—*Vivian A. Steiner, Moran, Michigan*

OIL AND VINEGAR DRESSINGS

★ ★

A 1942 Wesson oil ad helps an aproned wife escape "salad-sameness" with a "Quik-Change" recipe that offers a basic dressing recipe plus add-ins for different salads—pickle relish for green salad, honey for fruit salad, horseradish for mixed salads, and tomato juice for seafood salads. Here is a similar "quick change" for your salads.

¼ cup cider or wine vinegar
½ teaspoon dry mustard
½ teaspoon salt

½ teaspoon sugar
⅛ teaspoon ground white pepper
½ cup vegetable oil

Combine the vinegar, mustard, salt, sugar, and pepper in a ½-pint jar with a tight-fitting lid; cover and shake.

Add the oil; cover and shake well.

Variations: Add 3 tablespoons of any of the following—pickle relish, honey, horseradish, tomato juice—and shake until combined.

About ¾ Cup

WARTIME FRENCH DRESSING

★ ★

This idea comes from a little wartime booklet entitled "Successful Salads." It advises the home-maker that "chicken fat may be used in place of salad oils to make French dressing. The dressing must be stored in the refrigerator and warmed slightly to melt the chicken fat before each use." My grandmother used to render the fat that she removed from the large hens she bought for soups and stews. I never saw her use it for salad dressing, but she did use the fat for cooking or in her soft sugar cookies. This is a good all-purpose dressing even if you make it with vegetable oil.

1 teaspoon paprika	⅛ teaspoon ground black pepper
½ teaspoon dry mustard	¼ cup lemon juice or cider vinegar
½ teaspoon sugar	1 teaspoon finely grated onion
¼ teaspoon celery salt	½ cup melted chicken fat or
⅛ teaspoon garlic powder	vegetable oil

Stir together the paprika, mustard, sugar, celery salt, garlic powder, and pepper in a ½-pint jar with a tight-fitting lid. Add the lemon juice and onion; cover and shake. Add the chicken fat; cover and shake until combined.

About ¾ Cup

"If you are not salvaging your kitchen fats, begin now—this very day. Millions of pounds of waste fat are needed to produce the glycerin used in making gunpowder, and other munitions. A dangerous shortage threatens because many of you have been shirking this job."—*How to stretch your meat, butter and shortening,* 1943

WARTIME SPECIAL

Knox Spread

1 teaspoon unflavored gelatin	¼ teaspoon salt
1 tablespoon cold water	½ cup evaporated milk
¼ pound (1 stick) butter	Food coloring, optional

Sprinkle the gelatine over the cold water in a custard cup; set aside 5 minutes to soften. Set cup in pan of hot water and stir until gelatine has dissolved.

Cut butter into small chunks and warm over hot water until soft enough to beat, being careful not to melt the butter.

Add the gelatine mixture and salt to the milk. Gradually beat the milk mixture into the softened butter until the milk no longer separates.

Pack the mixture into a refrigerator dish and chill until firm.

This recipe ran in a Knox Gelatine advertisement in many magazines during the summer of 1943. It was well received by homemakers and is one of the kitchen tricks home-front cooks told me they remembered doing. The ad says, "You save 39 cents or more based on average prices."

½ Pound

APRICOT CORN BREAD

★ ★

Vitamin-rich dried apricots add to the nutrition packed into this low-fat breakfast, lunchbox, or dinner quick-bread.

1½ cups unsifted all-purpose flour
¾ cup cornmeal
2 tablespoons light brown sugar
3 teaspoons baking powder
½ teaspoon salt
¾ cup milk

2 large eggs
3 tablespoons vegetable shortening or
   butter (or a mixture), melted
½ cup dried apricot halves, finely
   chopped

Preheat oven to 350°F. Grease an 8-inch square baking pan.

Stir together flour, cornmeal, brown sugar, baking powder, and salt in a medium bowl. Combine milk, eggs, and melted shortening in a small bowl; add to dry ingredients and stir just until combined. Fold in apricots and spoon into greased pan.

Bake cornbread 25 to 30 minutes or until a toothpick inserted in the center comes out clean. Cool 10 minutes. Cut into 8 rectangles and serve warm.

8 Servings

LOW-FAT MUFFINS

★ ★

Based on a 1943 Swans Down cake flour ad, these muffins use cake flour to help provide the tenderness usually added by shortening.

1⅓ cups unsifted cake flour	⅔ cup milk
2 tablespoons light brown sugar	1 large egg, lightly beaten
2 teaspoons baking powder	1 tablespoon melted butter
¼ teaspoon salt	

Heat oven to 400°F. Grease an 8-cup muffin pan.

Combine flour, brown sugar, baking powder, and salt in a medium bowl. Beat together milk and egg in a small bowl.

Make a well in center of flour mixture. Add milk mixture and butter. Stir just until all dry ingredients have been moistened. Do not overbeat.

Divide muffin mixture into greased muffin cups and bake 20 to 22 minutes or until a toothpick inserted in the center of one comes out clean. Cool in pan 5 minutes. Remove to serving container and serve warm.

8 Muffins

"It takes about 100 pounds of milk to make 5 pounds of butter—or in other figures—9 to 10 quarts of milk to make a single pound. This relationship between butter and milk makes it easy to understand why both of them become such important commodities in wartime."—*American Cookery*, February 1944

SPOON BREAD

★ ★

Somewhere between a pudding and a bread, this Southern favorite can be dressed up for the holidays with the addition of coconut or converted to a main dish with the addition of some leftover ham. This fat-free version makes the most of the richness provided by the eggs.

1 cup yellow cornmeal	2 tablespoons light brown sugar
1 cup cold water	1 teaspoon baking powder
1 teaspoon salt	½ cup milk
1 cup boiling water	1 cup grated coconut or chopped
2 large eggs	ham, optional

Combine cornmeal, cold water, and salt in a 2-quart saucepan. Beat in boiling water until smooth. Bring mixture to a boil over medium heat, stirring constantly. Continue cooking and stirring 5 minutes. Set aside 15 minutes to cool slightly.

Preheat oven to 400°F. Lightly grease a 1½-quart casserole or baking dish. Meanwhile beat eggs at high speed until very light. Gradually beat in brown sugar until thick and light. Fold in baking powder.

When cornmeal mixture has cooled, beat in milk. Fold in beaten egg mixture until completely combined. Fold in coconut or ham, if desired.

Pour mixture into greased casserole and bake until puffed and firm, 35 to 40 minutes. Serve immediately.

6 Servings

BLUEBERRY COBBLER

★ ★

Fruit-based desserts such as this cobbler became popular because the seasonal fruit filling created most of the dessert and the thin layer of cake, biscuit, or pastry on top required only a little precious fat.

2 cups fresh or frozen blueberries

½ cup packed light brown sugar

1 tablespoon cornstarch

1¼ cups unsifted all-purpose flour

2 teaspoons baking powder

¼ teaspoon salt

¼ cup vegetable shortening or butter (or a mixture)

½ cup milk

1 large egg, lightly beaten

2 teaspoons vanilla extract

Preheat oven to 350°F. Grease an 8-inch square baking dish. Combine berries, 2 tablespoons brown sugar, and the cornstarch; spread out in greased pan.

Combine flour, remaining brown sugar, the baking powder, and salt in a medium bowl. Cut in shortening with a pastry blender or 2 knives until mixture forms fine crumbs.

Add milk, egg, and vanilla; stir just until combined. Spoon over berries.

Bake 30 to 35 minutes or until center springs back when lightly pressed. Cool 15 minutes. Cut into 6 rectangles and serve from pan.

6 Servings

"Rinse the fat out of cooking pans with a little hot water. Add to your soup kettle or use in gravy. Melt or scrape off any fats that cling to wrappings, or use the papers to grease pans, but don't forget fats for salvage. Keep your quota up!"—*Ladies' Home Journal*, October 1943

BROWN BETTY

★ ★

A flavorful combination of apples and fresh bread crumbs, this dessert is often made with lots of melted butter. This version uses butter just on top where it makes a crisp golden crumb layer, and is much lower in fat for the sacrifice.

2 cups day-old white bread crumbs
   (from 5 to 6 slices bread)
⅓ cup packed light brown sugar
1 teaspoon ground cinnamon
2 pounds cooking apples, peeled,
   cored, and thinly sliced

¼ cup orange juice
1 teaspoon butter, melted
Plain or whipped heavy cream,
   optional

Preheat oven to 400°F. Lightly grease a 1½-quart casserole or baking dish. Combine bread crumbs, brown sugar, and cinnamon.

Arrange one third of apples in bottom of casserole; top with one third of crumb mixture. Repeat once. Add remaining apples; drizzle orange juice over top. Combine remaining third of crumb mixture and butter; sprinkle evenly over top.

Bake until apples are tender, 40 to 45 minutes. Cool 15 to 20 minutes, then serve warm with cream, if desired.

6 Servings

"Fats are extremely important as an energy food. With less heat in our homes it becomes necessary to supply more body heat during the cold months."—69 *Ration Recipes for Meat*, undated

CHERRY PUDDING

★ ★

My grandmother and mother would serve this for supper on a day when we had had a big dinner at noon. Generous rectangles of the warm pudding would be served in a soup plate with milk to pour over it and that was the whole meal. It is best with fresh sour cherries, but we now freeze some cherries in season so we can have it all year round.

2 cups unsifted all-purpose flour

¾ cup packed light brown sugar

3 teaspoons baking powder

¼ teaspoon salt

½ cup milk

3 tablespoons vegetable shortening or
   butter (or a mixture), melted

1 large egg, lightly beaten

2 teaspoons vanilla extract

2 cups seeded fresh or very well
   drained frozen or canned cherries

Warm milk, optional

Preheat oven to 350°F. Grease an 8-inch square baking pan.

Combine flour, brown sugar, baking powder, and salt in a medium bowl. Add milk, shortening, egg, and vanilla; stir just until combined. Fold in cherries and pour into greased pan.

Bake 25 to 30 minutes or until center springs back when lightly pressed. Cool 15 minutes. Cut into 6 rectangles and serve warm from pan with warm milk to pour over it, if desired.

6 Servings

WARTIME SPECIAL

Butterless Butter

1 envelope gelatin

1 tablespoon cold water

3 tablespoons boiling water

⅓ cup evaporated milk

⅓ cup mayonnaise

¼ teaspoon salt

½ pound margarine, softened

Soften gelatin in cold water; add boiling water and stir until dissolved. Stir in milk, then mayonnaise and salt; chill until thickened. Beat softened margarine. Gradually beat in mayonnaise mixture; spoon into a covered container and refrigerate.

"Altho' raised in a small town, and having a maid to do the cooking, I was very inexperienced in this field, but you do what you have to do! My husband bought a cow—I learned to churn my butter—(he milked the cow) and I learned to can 450 quarts of food from his garden." *Katherine G. Moore, Amelia, Virginia*

APPLESAUCE CAKE

★ ★

My wartime baby-sitter, Aunt Sue, was an Applesauce Cake specialist. The spicy aroma of the cake baking so enticed me that when my mother came for me I would refuse to go home until I was given a slice of cake to take with me. Even when I was very grown up, Aunt Sue always brought me an applesauce cake for my birthday. The cake was different from year to year because she always made it from her home-canned applesauce, which varied depending upon the variety of apples she had used to make it. This is as close as I can get to the cake I remember.

1¾ cups unsifted all-purpose flour
1 teaspoon baking soda
1 teaspoon ground cinnamon
½ teaspoon salt
¼ teaspoon ground mace
⅛ teaspoon ground cloves

½ cup packed light brown sugar
⅓ cup vegetable shortening or
   softened butter (or a mixture)
2 large eggs
1⅓ cups unsweetened applesauce
½ cup dark seedless raisins

Preheat oven to 350°F. Grease two 8-inch round baking pans. Stir together flour, baking soda, cinnamon, salt, mace, and cloves.

Beat together brown sugar and shortening until fluffy. Beat in eggs. Fold in applesauce and flour mixture until just combined; then fold in raisins.

Spoon mixture into greased pans and bake 25 to 30 minutes or until a toothpick inserted in center of each comes out clean.

Cool 5 minutes in pans, then remove to wire racks to cool completely.

10 Servings

BREAD CRUMB COOKIES

★ ★

During the war there was no shortage of recipes using day-old bread. In this quick cookie, the bread crumbs take the place of flour. Never substitute commercial dry bread crumbs for the moister homemade day-old ones.

2 large eggs

¼ teaspoon salt

½ cup packed light brown sugar

2 cups day-old white bread crumbs (from 5 to 6 slices bread)

1 cup finely chopped walnuts

½ teaspoon vanilla extract

Preheat oven to 375°F. Grease 2 baking sheets.

Beat eggs and salt with an electric mixer on high speed until very light. Gradually beat in brown sugar until fluffy. Fold in bread crumbs, walnuts, and vanilla.

Drop dough by rounded measuring teaspoonfuls onto greased baking sheets and bake 10 to 12 minutes or until golden and centers are set. Cool and serve or pack in an airtight container.

48 Cookies

Coloring Margarine

"Use a big bowl when you color the margarine. Soften to room temperature—important! Do not heat—you'll destroy its texture. Put on the coloring. Work in easily with blending fork or wooden spoon. This lady's using her pet potato masher—just the ticket. Two minutes and the job's all done."—*Better Homes and Gardens*, December 1943

CRUMB CAKE

★ ★

This has been one of our family's favorite recipes as long as I can remember. I used to take cupcakes made from this recipe to school for my birthday celebrations.

1¾ cups unsifted all-purpose flour

¾ cup packed light brown sugar

1 teaspoon ground cinnamon

¼ teaspoon ground nutmeg

¼ teaspoon salt

¼ teaspoon ground cloves

⅓ cup vegetable shortening or butter
 (or a mixture)

2 teaspoons baking powder

1 cup milk

1 large egg, lightly beaten

Preheat oven to 350°F. Grease and flour an 8-inch square baking pan.

Combine flour, brown sugar, cinnamon, nutmeg, salt, and cloves in a medium bowl. Cut in shortening with a pastry blender or 2 knives until mixture forms fine crumbs. Set aside ½ cup crumb mixture.

Stir baking powder into remaining flour mixture. Add milk and egg and stir just until combined. Transfer to greased and floured pan and top with reserved crumbs.

Bake 30 to 35 minutes or until center springs back when lightly pressed. Cool 15 minutes. Cut into 8 rectangles and serve from pan.

8 Servings

DUTCH APPLE CAKE

★ ★

Dutch Apple Cake appears in many wartime baking articles, with many variations. I like this upside-down version best because the apples are baked under the cake and really become tender. This recipe originally called for 1 tablespoon heavy cream in the topping. In those days, with a delicious layer of cream at the top of every milk bottle, that wasn't hard to come by. I have changed it to milk so you don't have to buy a half-pint of cream to get 1 tablespoon, but if you have some cream in the refrigerator feel free to use it.

1 tablespoon butter	3 tablespoons granulated sugar
⅓ cup packed brown sugar	3 teaspoons baking powder
1 tablespoon plus 1 cup milk	½ teaspoon salt
1 teaspoon ground cinnamon	¼ cup vegetable shortening or butter
2 cups sliced apples	(or a mixture)
1¾ cups unsifted all-purpose flour	1 large egg, beaten

Preheat oven to 375°F. Melt butter in an 8-inch square baking pan. Stir in brown sugar, 1 tablespoon milk, and the cinnamon. Arrange apple slices in brown sugar mixture.

Combine flour, granulated sugar, baking powder, and salt in a medium bowl. Add shortening and cut into flour mixture with pastry blender or 2 knives to make coarse crumbs. Add remaining ¾ cup milk and the egg; stir together until a soft dough forms. Spoon dough over apples.

Bake cake 40 to 45 minutes or until center springs back when gently pressed. Remove from oven; immediately loosen edges of cake and invert onto a heatproof serving plate. Serve warm.

6 Servings

WAR CAKE

★ ★

This recipe was handwritten in the back of a recipe pamphlet dating from the first decade of the 1900s. It is similar to recipes that appeared in the 1940s as well as to those from Civil War times. In each case, boiled raisins were an important part of the recipe. This cake keeps well, travels well, and is an excellent alternative to holiday fruit cake.

1 pound raisins

2 cups packed light brown sugar

2 cups water

4 tablespoons lard or vegetable shortening

2 teaspoons salt

2 teaspoons ground cinnamon

½ teaspoon ground cloves

3 cups unsifted all-purpose flour

2 teaspoons baking soda

Combine raisins, brown sugar, water, lard, salt, cinnamon, and cloves in a 2-quart saucepan. Bring to a boil over medium heat; cook 5 minutes, stirring occasionally. Cool to room temperature.

Preheat oven to 350°F. Grease a 10-inch tube pan. Stir together flour and baking soda.

Fold dry ingredients into cooled raisin mixture. Spoon into greased pan and bake 45 to 50 minutes or until a toothpick inserted in center comes out clean.

Cool 5 minutes in pan, then invert onto a wire rack to cool completely.

12 Servings

WHIPPED CREAM CAKE

★ ★

The use of heavy cream in this recipe solves the butter problem, but the recipe does call for 1 cup granulated sugar—a ration-time challenge. The elegant cake that results would be perfect for a wedding cake.

2 cups sifted cake flour (sift before measuring)

3 teaspoons baking powder

¼ teaspoon salt

3 large eggs

1 cup sugar

1 cup heavy cream

1 teaspoon vanilla extract

½ teaspoon almond extract

Sugarless Boiled Frosting (page 97)

Preheat oven to 350°F. Grease two 9-inch round baking pans. Stir together flour, baking powder, and salt.

Beat eggs with electric mixer set at high speed, gradually adding sugar until mixture is thick and fluffy. With same beaters, beat cream, vanilla, and almond extract just until soft peaks form. Gently fold eggs and then dry ingredients into whipped cream mixture until smooth.

Divide batter into greased pans and bake 25 to 30 minutes or until a toothpick inserted in the center of each layer comes out clean. Cool, then fill and frost.

10 Servings

8

FOODS TO PACK

★★★★★★★★★★★★★★★★★★★★★

Split Pea Soup	Ham Turnovers
Butter Noodle Soup	Orange Raisin Nut Bread
Ham and Grated Carrot Salad	Butterscotch Cupcakes
Green Bean and Egg Salad	Candy-Bar Cookies
Baked Bean Sandwiches	Chocolate Coconut Macaroons
Liver and Bacon Sandwiches	Chocolate Walnut Drops
Mom's "Ham" Salad Sandwiches	Molasses Hermits
Cream Cheese and Olive Sandwiches	Spiced Nuts

Send
C-Mail
to the Wounded
Over Here!

C-MAIL IS CHEER MAIL...
COOKIES, CAKES, CHOCOLATE

Uncle Sam's boys are well fed—no matter where they are.

But convalescent men, in hospital beds or wheel chairs, long for homemade sweets.

Send these homesick wounded a *real* taste of home. Cookies, for instance, that take them back to little-boyhood...that set them dreaming of sunny kitchens ...Mom's Saturday bakings.

A *little* of your time will make a *lot* of happy time for them. Nothing will be so appreciated...nothing can so well show *your* appreciation of what they've done for you.

You know, of course, how soldiers go for Cookies. They love 'em! So be sure your C-Mail includes a generous quantity of various kinds.

A man doesn't have to be wounded to enjoy Toll House Cookies. But if he is, these golden, crunchy cookies made with Nestle's Semi-Sweet Chocolate are doubly precious, doubly good.

Chocolate is a fighting food. So if your dealer is temporarily short of Nestle's Semi-Sweet ask him to save you some when he gets it.

Send *C-Mail* Over Here
...*V-Mail* Over There

Not only was it necessary for wartime homemakers to pack lunches for themselves to take to defense jobs and for their children to carry to school, but many homemakers also participated in government-supported community programs, in which they produced thousands of sandwiches for troops being moved around the country or arriving home by ship. In addition, magazines frequently carried articles suggesting that sweets from home were the very best present to send to servicemen both in the United States and abroad.

As soon as America went to war, lunch box packing became a creative endeavor. Homemakers were reminded that the future of the country was in their hands as they packed lunches for family members to take to their defense jobs and children to take to school. Lunches had to meet government nutrition guidelines, stay safe and palatable when stored at room temperature for four or more hours, complement the other meals in the day, provide daily variety, be convenient to eat, and please the person for whom it had been packed—a big order. The accepted formula was to include either hot soup or a nutritious hot drink in a thermos bottle; two different high-protein sandwiches on whole-grain bread; crisp fresh vegetables; a cupcake, cookie, turnover, or other sweet; and a piece of fresh fruit. Sandwich fillings incorporated bits of meat or cheese with a wide variety of chopped or grated fresh vegetables. Workers might open their lunch box to find Liverwurst and Celery, Bologna and Cabbage, Ham and Cucumber, Cheese and Nut, Peanut Butter and Orange, Dried-Beef and Cheese, or Bacon and Celery Spread Sandwiches for variety.

Homemakers needed help with their new lunch box responsibilities, and the food departments of women's magazines immediately offered assistance. The Good Housekeeping Institute experimented with sandwich fillings and recommended that sandwiches could be made in the evening and refrigerated overnight to save time in the morning. The same precision went into their testing of cookie recipes to be shipped abroad. Cookies were packed using their special packing instructions, shipped 2,000 miles, and then tasted.

The first part of this chapter offers the components of generously packed lunches—soup, salads, sandwiches, and portable pastries, while treats that travel without crumbling (in boxes filled with homemade popcorn) complete the selection.

SPLIT PEA SOUP

★ ★

Soup is the original easy, thrifty, satisfying solution to sustenance during difficult times. When people worked long hours at active jobs, they needed something both nutritious and comforting in their lunch box. This soup can be made ahead, refrigerated, and warmed in the morning to fill a thermos.

2 cups split green or yellow peas

¼ pound salt pork or bacon, finely chopped

1 cup chopped onions

8 cups water

½ to 1 teaspoon salt

½ teaspoon ground black pepper

1 cup milk

2 tablespoons all-purpose flour

Pick through peas and discard any discolored ones or foreign material; rinse thoroughly. Heat salt pork in 5-quart Dutch oven or soup pot until it releases some fat. Add onions and sauté until pork and onions start to brown. Add water, peas, ½ teaspoon salt, and the pepper. Bring to a boil over high heat; reduce heat to low, cover, and simmer, stirring occasionally until peas are very tender, 50 to 60 minutes.

Beat milk into flour with a wire whisk until smooth. Gradually beat mixture into soup. Bring to a boil and cook, stirring 1 minute or until slightly thickened. Taste and add additional salt, if necessary.

Serve, or cool to room temperature, cover, and refrigerate until ready to use. Heat one serving at a time and serve or use to fill a thermos.

6 Servings

BUTTER NOODLE SOUP

This was always one of my favorite lunches as a child. Perhaps not very nutritious, but warm, filling, and easy to make with what was on hand.

1 cup water

¼ teaspoon dried parsley leaves

¼ teaspoon salt

¼ cup thin egg noodles

1 teaspoon butter, or more if you have it

Bring water, parsley, and salt to a boil over high heat. Stir in noodles and butter and return to a boil. Reduce heat to low and cook until noodles are just tender, 8 to 10 minutes.

Pour through a funnel into a thermos bottle or spoon into a bowl and serve.

1 Serving

HAM AND GRATED CARROT SALAD

★ ★

Salad is a nice alternative to sandwiches for lunch. It can be packed in a paper cup, covered with a double layer of wax paper that is held in place with a rubber band. The addition of some cubes of leftover ham to this classic salad makes it a good main dish for a packed lunch.

2 tablespoons mayonnaise

1 tablespoon corn syrup

1 tablespoon finely chopped green
   bell pepper

⅛ teaspoon ground black pepper

2 cups coarsely grated carrots

½ cup cooked ham, cut into ½-inch
   pieces

4 leaves lettuce, rinsed and crisped,
   optional

Combine the mayonnaise, corn syrup, bell pepper, and black pepper in a medium bowl. Fold in carrots and ham.

Divide carrot mixture onto 4 salad plates lined with lettuce, if desired, or pack for lunch box.

4 Servings

> "Include in every lunch box the essentials of a well balanced meal: protein such as eggs, fish, cheese or meat; milk in some form, vegetables, fruits and enriched bread or other whole grain cereal. This will insure the luncher against deficiencies of vitamins, minerals and proteins so necessary for vigorous bodies and active minds."—*Coupon Cookery*, 1943

GREEN BEAN AND EGG SALAD

★ ★

Green beans were a popular backyard crop and produced abundantly in most climates. This fresh green bean salad would be a welcome surprise in a worker's lunch box. The oil and vinegar dressing on page 155 would be good here.

½ pound green beans, trimmed and
   cut diagonally crosswise
¼ teaspoon salt

¼ cup oil and vinegar dressing
1 green onion, finely chopped
2 hard-cooked large eggs, chilled

Combine beans, salt, and water to just cover in a heavy saucepan. Bring to a boil over high heat; reduce heat to low, cover, and simmer until just tender, about 5 minutes. Drain well.

Combine cooked beans, oil and vinegar dressing, and green onion in a small bowl. Cover and refrigerate at least 1 hour or until ready to pack or serve.

To pack or serve, peel eggs; cut each into 8 pieces and mix with beans. Divide between 2 containers or salad plates.

2 Servings

"War-working lunches must offer good square meals, appealing each day."—*Recipes for Today*, 1943

BAKED BEAN SANDWICHES

My mother remembers having baked bean sandwiches when she was in college before the war. So, this was not a new idea but one that met perfectly the need for nutritious meatless sandwich fillings. All commercially canned baked beans went to the armed forces during the war, so homemade ones were the only choice for these sandwiches.

2 cups your favorite baked beans,
    cold, see Note
2 tablespoons very finely chopped
    onion

2 tablespoons ketchup
8 slices firm white bread
4 leaves lettuce, rinsed and crisped
2 tablespoons mayonnaise

Mash the beans and stir in onion and ketchup. Divide mixture on 4 slices of bread. Spread to reach crusts. Top each with a lettuce leaf. Spread mayonnaise over remaining bread slices and place them on top of first 4 slices. Cut in half diagonally and serve or wrap for lunch box.

4 Servings

NOTE: Homemade baked beans are still the best choice because they chill to a spreadable consistency. If you are using canned ones, drain them very well, or simmer them until the liquid evaporates then chill them.

Cheer for Lunch Boxes

WARTIME SPECIAL

Chicken Salad Spread

½ cup chicken broth

4½ teaspoons instant tapioca

¼ teaspoon salt

⅛ teaspoon ground black
  pepper

⅛ teaspoon paprika

½ cup finely chopped chicken

2 tablespoons finely chopped
  celery

2 tablespoons pickle relish

2 tablespoons mayonnaise

1 teaspoon cider vinegar

Combine broth, tapioca, salt, pepper, and paprika in a small saucepan. Bring to a boil over high heat, stirring constantly. Remove from heat and stir in chicken, celery, relish, mayonnaise, and vinegar.

Transfer to a small bowl, cool to room temperature; cover and refrigerate until ready to use.

1 Cup Spread

LIVER AND BACON SANDWICHES

★ ★

This is representative of the many sandwich fillings made by chopping or grinding meats or vegetables and combining them with mayonnaise to make a spread.

4 strips bacon

½ pound liver (beef, pork, or lamb), cut into 1-inch strips

¼ cup finely chopped onion

3 tablespoons mayonnaise

1 tablespoon pickle relish or finely chopped stuffed green olives

¼ teaspoon salt

¼ teaspoon ground black pepper

8 slices rye bread

4 leaves lettuce, rinsed and crisped

Sauté the bacon until crisp in a large skillet. Remove bacon; drain well, reserving drippings in skillet. Sauté the liver and onion in bacon drippings, until liver is just cooked through, 5 to 8 minutes.

Grind liver and onion together with a food grinder (or processor). Crumble bacon. Combine the ground liver mixture with bacon, 2 tablespoons mayonnaise, the pickle relish, salt, and pepper.

Divide mixture onto 4 slices of bread. Spread to reach crusts. Top each with a lettuce leaf. Spread remaining 1 tablespoon mayonnaise over remaining bread slices and place them on top of first 4 slices. Cut in half diagonally and serve or wrap for lunch box.

4 Servings

MOM'S "HAM" SALAD SANDWICHES

★ ★

If you grind that infamous canned spiced pork product and add enough extra ingredients no one will notice that it isn't ham. When I was in college, my mother made dozens of these for parties and everyone loved them.

1 (12-ounce) can spiced pork
   luncheon meat, coarsely chopped
2 hard-cooked large eggs
4 (3-inch) sweet pickles
6 tablespoons cooked salad dressing

   or mayonnaise
2 teaspoons yellow mustard
12 slices firm white bread
6 leaves lettuce, rinsed and crisped

Grind or process luncheon meat, eggs, and pickles until fine. Stir in 4 tablespoons salad dressing and the mustard.

Divide mixture onto 4 slices of bread. Spread to reach crusts. Top each with a lettuce leaf. Spread remaining 2 tablespoons salad dressing over remaining bread slices and place them on top of first 4 slices. Cut in half diagonally and serve or wrap for lunch box.

6 Servings

"Due to my own experiments, I was able to make foods my husband could take to the field with him, no refrigeration, to keep, share and enjoy with comrades to supplement their C-rations."—*Ozelda H. Havens, Beaumont, Texas*

CREAM CHEESE AND OLIVE SANDWICHES

★ ★

Cream cheese was a popular sandwich filling because it was a congenial complement to whatever was on hand.

2 (3-ounce) packages cream cheese, softened

1 tablespoon mayonnaise

1 tablespoon milk

⅛ teaspoon ground black pepper

2 tablespoons finely chopped stuffed green olives

1 tablespoon very finely chopped green onion

8 slices firm white bread

½ cup thinly sliced iceberg lettuce

1 or 2 teaspoons butter, softened

Combine cream cheese, mayonnaise, milk, and pepper in a small bowl. Fold in olives and green onion. Divide mixture onto 4 slices of bread. Spread to reach crusts. Top each with one quarter of the lettuce. Spread butter over remaining bread slices and place them on top of first 4 slices. Cut in half diagonally and serve or wrap for lunch box.

4 Servings

"The Victory Lunch Box Meal: Hearty, wholesome, combats fatigue, maintains efficiency on the job, interesting and appetizing, varied daily. . . . Take a peek before you close the cover. Would you want to eat the contents 5 hours later?"—*Your Share*, 1943

HAM TURNOVERS

These stuffed biscuits make a nice alternative to daily sandwiches. They can be baked the night before and refrigerated until ready to pack in the morning.

½ cup finely chopped cooked ham

2 tablespoons pickle relish

1 tablespoon milk

2 teaspoons prepared mustard

1 cup unsifted all-purpose flour

1½ teaspoons baking powder

¼ teaspoon salt

3 tablespoons vegetable shortening or butter (or a mixture)

⅓ cup milk

Stir together ham, pickle relish, milk, and mustard in a small bowl; set aside. Preheat oven to 375°F. Grease a baking sheet.

Combine flour, baking powder, and salt in a medium bowl. Cut in shortening with a pastry blender or 2 knives until mixture forms fine crumbs. Add milk and stir together. Roll out to a 16-inch square on a floured board. Cut into 4 (4-inch) squares. Divide ham mixture onto biscuit squares. Moisten edges of squares and fold over to make each into a triangle. Press edges together and transfer to baking sheet. Pierce center of each with tines of a fork.

Bake turnovers until golden brown and firm, 15 to 20 minutes. Serve warm or cool to room temperature, wrap, and refrigerate to pack in lunch boxes.

4 Servings

ORANGE RAISIN NUT BREAD

★ ★

This sweet tea bread makes good cream cheese or peanut butter and jelly sandwiches. By itself, it is a satisfying breakfast.

1½ cups unsifted all-purpose flour
½ cup unsifted whole-wheat flour
½ cup packed light brown sugar
4 teaspoons baking powder
1 teaspoon finely grated orange peel
¼ teaspoon salt

1 cup orange juice
1 large egg, lightly beaten
¼ cup salad oil or melted vegetable shortening
½ cup dark seedless raisins
½ cup chopped nuts

Preheat oven to 350°F. Grease a 9-inch loaf pan.

Combine all-purpose flour, whole-wheat flour, brown sugar, baking powder, orange peel, and salt in a large bowl. Beat together orange juice, egg, and oil in a small bowl. Add liquid ingredients to dry ingredients and stir just until no flour shows. Fold in raisins and nuts. Transfer stiff batter to greased loaf pan.

Bake 55 to 60 minutes or until a toothpick inserted in center comes out clean. Cool to room temperature and serve or pack in an airtight container.

12 Servings

BUTTERSCOTCH CUPCAKES

★ ★

This is the cupcake recipe I have been hunting for ever since I learned to cook. I remember the flavor from a childhood birthday party and could never find a recipe that was quite right until I tested this one based on an idea in a magazine article about coping with the shortage of white granulated sugar. Using all brown sugar is the secret to these one-bowl cupcakes. But alas, they should all be eaten on the day they are baked or they are not as good.

1½ cups unsifted cake flour	2 large eggs
1½ teaspoons baking powder	½ cup milk
¼ teaspoon salt	1 teaspoon vanilla extract
1 cup packed light brown sugar	Chocolate Frosting (recipe follows)
⅓ cup vegetable shortening or butter (or a mixture)	

Preheat oven to 350°F. Grease a 12-cup cupcake pan. Stir together flour, baking powder, and salt; set aside.

Beat together brown sugar and shortening until fluffy. Beat in eggs one at a time.

Add dry ingredients to sugar mixture along with milk and vanilla. Beat just until smooth.

Divide batter into the greased cupcake cups and bake 20 to 25 minutes or until a toothpick inserted in center of one comes out clean. Cool and frost.

CHOCOLATE FROSTING: Stir together 1½ cups confectioners' sugar, 1 melted (1-ounce) square unsweetened chocolate, 2 tablespoons vegetable shortening, 1 to 2 tablespoons milk, and ½ teaspoon vanilla extract until smooth.

12 Cupcakes

WARTIME SPECIAL

Victory Sandwiches

2½ cups cooked string beans, finely chopped

2 tablespoons mayonnaise

2 tablespoons finely chopped parsley

¼ teaspoon dried basil

¼ teaspoon dried thyme

½ teaspoon salt

⅛ teaspoon ground black pepper

Drain beans well and chop very fine. Add remaining ingredients and blend. Makes 1 cup and fills 5 or 6 full-size sandwiches.

5 or 6 Servings

"In the dead of winter, my mother sent me by parcel post, a dressed-out and salted-down to retard spoilage, five-pound chicken! Pure heaven! With a pound of home-made butter . . ."—*Loretta Holmes, Beloit, Wisconsin*

CANDY-BAR COOKIES

★ ★

A May 1942 Baby Ruth candy bar advertisement declared the popular candy bar "Energy Food for Victory." They certainly are a yummy addition to these cookies. The ad reminds moms and sweethearts to bake the cookies and "Send him a box of them today."

1½ cups unsifted all-purpose flour

½ teaspoon baking soda

¼ teaspoon salt

½ cup vegetable shortening or butter (or a mixture)

½ cup packed light brown sugar

1 large egg

1 teaspoon vanilla extract

2 (2.1-ounce) chocolate-covered peanut, caramel nougat candy bars, cut into ½-inch pieces

Preheat oven to 375°F. Grease 2 baking sheets. Stir together flour, baking soda, and salt; set aside.

Beat together shortening and brown sugar in a medium bowl until fluffy. Beat in egg and vanilla. Stir in dry ingredients and candy bar pieces.

Drop dough by rounded teaspoonfuls onto greased baking sheets and bake 8 to 10 minutes or until cookies are golden and centers are set. Cool and serve or pack in an airtight container.

36 Cookies

CHOCOLATE COCONUT MACAROONS

★ ★

Sometimes called Jiffy Cookies, this recipe met the wartime cook's need for speed, simplicity, and a guaranteed successful and delicious outcome. The fact that the cookies keep and ship well is a plus. The basic combination of sweetened condensed milk and coconut had been promoted by the sweetened condensed milk manufacturer for some time. Wartime bakers created variations with the addition of dried fruit, nuts, and spices, as well as chocolate.

4 cups sweetened grated coconut
1 (14-ounce) can sweetened
**   condensed milk**

3 ounces unsweetened chocolate,
**   melted**
1 teaspoon vanilla extract

Preheat oven to 350°F. Grease 2 baking sheets well. Combine coconut, sweetened condensed milk, chocolate, and vanilla in a large bowl, mixing well.

Drop by teaspoonfuls, about 1 inch apart, onto baking sheets. Bake just until firm and tips of coconut have started to brown, about 10 minutes. Remove to cooling rack immediately.

36 Cookies

"If it (your box of cookies) is going to a boy in camp at holiday time, plan to have it arrive either before or after the holiday. Our armed forces always are served real holiday meals, and even a box from home loses some of its appeal after two or more helpings of a bountiful feast."—*Good Housekeeping*, December 1942

CHOCOLATE WALNUT DROPS

A 1944 Nestlé ad reminds home bakers that "Chocolate is a fighting food" and that temporary shortages may occur. Despite that possibility, chocolate dessert recipes continued to appear regularly in magazines.

1⅔ cups unsifted all-purpose flour

1 teaspoon baking powder

¼ teaspoon salt

½ cup vegetable shortening or butter (or a mixture)

½ cup packed light brown sugar

½ cup dark corn syrup

2 ounces unsweetened chocolate, melted

1 large egg

1 teaspoon vanilla extract

¾ cup chopped walnuts

Preheat oven to 350°F. Grease 2 baking sheets. Stir together flour, baking powder, and salt; set aside.

Beat together shortening and brown sugar in a medium bowl until fluffy. Gradually beat in corn syrup and chocolate, then egg and vanilla. Stir in dry ingredients until no flour shows. Fold in walnuts.

Drop dough by rounded teaspoonfuls onto greased baking sheets, 1 inch apart. Bake 10 to 12 minutes or until edges begin to brown and centers are set. Cool and serve or pack in an airtight container.

48 Cookies

MOLASSES HERMITS

★ ★

These spicy cookies were very popular in the early 1940s because the ingredients were not hard to come by and the moist spicy cookies were known to ship well. Magazine articles advised bakers packing boxes to be shipped overseas to wrap cookies in long wax paper tubes and surround them with homemade popcorn to prevent breakage. The popcorn was a tasty addition to the present as well.

1½ cups unsifted all-purpose flour	⅓ cup packed light brown sugar
1½ teaspoons baking powder	¼ cup light molasses
1½ teaspoons ground cinnamon	1 large egg
½ teaspoon ground nutmeg	¼ cup cold coffee or water
¼ teaspoon salt	½ teaspoon vanilla extract
⅓ cup vegetable shortening or butter	½ cup dark seedless raisins
(or a mixture)	½ cup chopped nuts, optional

Preheat oven to 375°F. Grease 2 baking sheets. Stir together flour, baking powder, cinnamon, nutmeg, and salt and set aside.

Beat together shortening, brown sugar, and molasses until fluffy. Beat in egg.

Stir in dry ingredients along with coffee and vanilla until no flour shows. Fold in raisins and nuts, if desired.

Drop batter by rounded teaspoonfuls onto greased baking sheets and bake 10 to 12 minutes or until a toothpick inserted in the center of one comes out clean. Cool and serve or pack in an airtight container.

36 Cookies

SPICED NUTS

★ ★

A coating of sugar and spice turns undressed nuts into an elegant gift. This easy recipe was appreciated by busy home-front cooks because they could create something special for a last-minute gift or for one extra package in a box that was going overseas.

⅔ cup packed light brown sugar

⅓ cup water

2 tablespoons corn syrup

⅛ teaspoon salt

1 teaspoon vanilla extract

½ teaspoon ground cinnamon

⅛ teaspoon ground allspice

1⅓ cups mixed unsalted roasted nuts

Lightly oil an aluminum-foil-lined baking sheet.

Bring brown sugar, water, corn syrup, and salt to a boil over high heat, stirring until sugar dissolves. Reduce heat to medium and cook without stirring until the syrup registers 236°F on a candy thermometer.

Remove syrup from heat and stir in vanilla, cinnamon, and allspice. Fold in nuts and spread mixture out as thin as possible on the prepared baking sheet. Cool, break into pieces, and store in an airtight container.

6 (¼-cup) Servings

"Plan for the lunch box when you're choosing the rest of the next day's meals. Then its contents will not only round out the other meals, but make good use of foods left from previous meals."—*Good Housekeeping,* June 1942

9

WARTIME ENTERTAINING

★ ★ ★ ★ ★ ★ ★ ★ ★ ★ ★ ★ ★ ★ ★ ★ ★ ★ ★ ★

Waffle Cheese Sandwiches

Mock Pâté de Fois Gras

Brisket with Vegetables

Giant Cheese "Hot Dogs"

Hungarian Goulash

Individual Lamb Roasts

Javanese Corn with Coconut

Oat Sticks

Potato Cloverleaf Rolls

Raised Chocolate Cake

Chocolate Spanish Cream

Strawberry or Raspberry Trifle

Flaky Pastry

Carrot Pie

Rhubarb Pie

Chocolate Marshmallow Pie

THE BASIC SEVEN FOOD GROUPS

EAT SOMETHING FROM EACH GROUP EVERY DAY

EATING RIGHT KEEPS YOU HEALTHY

IN ADDITION TO THE BASIC 7 ... EAT ANY OTHER FOODS YOU WANT

U. S. GOVERNMENT CHART

GROUP ONE

GROUP TWO

GROUP THREE

GROUP FOUR

GROUP FIVE

GROUP SIX

GROUP SEVEN

BUTTER AND FORTIFIED MARGARINE (with added Vitamin A)

GREEN AND YELLOW VEGETABLES... some raw—some cooked, frozen or canned

ORANGES, TOMATOES, GRAPEFRUIT... or raw cabbage or salad greens

POTATOES AND OTHER VEGETABLES AND FRUITS raw, dried, cooked, frozen or canned

BREAD, FLOUR, AND CEREALS... Natural whole grain—or enriched or restored

MEAT, POULTRY, FISH, OR EGGS... or dried beans, peas, nuts, or peanut butter

MILK AND MILK PRODUCTS... fluid, evaporated, dried milk or cheese

U.S. NEEDS US STRONG

EAT THE BASIC 7 EVERY DAY

Around this symbol is built the chart that gives the rules for proper nutrition based on conclusions as to normal human requirements as established by the Food and Nutrition Board of the National Research Council.

Entertaining was an important part of the 1940s' social scene. The December 1941 issue of *McCall's*, which was most likely written in late August but arrived to subscribers just days before the Japanese bombing of Pearl Harbor, showed young women discussing their favorite hand lotion at a "Defense Party." The media never suggested that entertaining be put on hold; rather, they offered strategies for presenting a socially acceptable spread within the confines of rationing and scarcity. One popular idea was the progressive party. If everyone served a course, the strain on ration books and pocketbooks would be shared. Families were encouraged to entertain servicemen stationed in their area and home entertaining for couples was heavily promoted.

Holiday entertaining was encouraged as good for the morale of the country. In a November 1942 article, "Thanksgiving, Don't skip it this year," *Good Housekeeping* editors offered a full turkey dinner plus a Thanksgiving Night Snack that included Spicy-Ham Spread, Shrimp-Salad Spread, Cottage-Cheese Temptation, and Peanut-Butter Spread with toast and fruit. An article in *Woman's Home Companion* the same month, entitled "For a New Kind of Thanksgiving," proposes "Let's Use a Simple Menu." And here it is:

Roast Turkey — Celery, Onion Stuffing
Old-Fashioned Cranberry Sauce
Fluffy Mashed Potatoes — Gravy
Honeyed Squash Squares
Wine or Apple Juice
Polka Dot Lemon Chiffon Pie
Deviled Nuts — Coffee

The photographs show that the family invited sailors from a neighboring camp and that they all packed a box including some of the nonperishable components of the meal to send to their boy, who was too far away to come home. Although the meal certainly doesn't sound like deprivation, the editors note that the table, "though short on courses is long on shining silver and Grandmother's china. No ration on hospitality and grace."

Good Housekeeping's December 1942 article, "Plan Your Holiday Meals This Way and

You'll Meet Uncle Sam's Recommendations for Nutritious Meals," explains to homemakers that many foods will be unavailable for holiday meals, but "you still will find such a wide variety in foods on the grocer's shelves that you easily can choose substitutes." And, to prove it, they plan the following menu:

Cranberry-Juice Cocktail
Carrot-Cheese Hors d'Oeuvres
Roast Turkey — Sweet Potato Stuffing
Giblet or Mushroom Gravy
Brussels Sprouts with Onions
String-Bean Succotash
Celery — Pickles — Pickled Fruit
Enriched Bread
Steamed Christmas Puddings — Strawberry Sauce
Roasted Walnuts — Coffee

The other occasion that captured the attention of women's magazines was the wartime wedding. Usually planned quickly and carried out inexpensively, they were more likely to be high on style and light on refreshments. A June 1943 *Good Housekeeping* article tells war brides, "you can marry in haste and have a wedding party, too!" The buffet reception consists of Chicken and Vegetable Aspic, Rolls or Biscuits, Jam, a Three-Tiered Cake, and Strawberry Punch. The menu for a sit-down affair is Asparagus Newburg, Watercress, Celery, and Radish Garnish, Fruit Sherbet, and Bride's Angel Food.

The recipes that follow are based on ones selected from entertaining menus that appeared in magazines and cookbooks of the period. Entertaining articles were usually focused on desserts and my choices are as well.

WAFFLE CHEESE SANDWICHES

★ ★

This makes a good party appetizer or snack. The sandwiches can be toasted on the buffet table with your guests in attendance or prepared ahead, refrigerated, and then crisped in a 350°F oven just before serving.

¼ pound American cheese, finely grated

1 tablespoon finely chopped drained pimiento

1 teaspoon mayonnaise

8 thin slices firm white bread

1 tablespoon margarine or butter, softened

Mix cheese, pimiento, and mayonnaise together with a fork until combined.

Trim crusts from bread. Spread 4 slices with cheese mixture and top with remaining bread slices to make 4 sandwiches. Spread outsides of sandwiches with margarine.

Preheat waffle iron. Toast each sandwich until golden. Cut toasted sandwiches into quarters and serve immediately or keep whole sandwiches warm until all have been toasted, quarter and serve. If desired, make and toast several hours ahead, refrigerate, covered. Warm 10 minutes in a 350°F oven before serving.

4 Servings

"All of us are mighty glad that our servicemen are getting first choice of America's food supplies for their holiday dinners. Yet there will still be meat for us at home. So invite your family and friends to gather round."—*Armour and Company advertisement,* December 1943

MOCK PÂTÉ DE FOIE GRAS

McCall's *magazine suggested a spread similar to this one with the subtitle "Luxury on a ration-stamp shoestring!" Although not really very much like pâté de foie gras it is still a very good appetizer spread.*

1 teaspoon butter
½ pound beef liver, cut into 1-inch
  pieces
2 tablespoons finely chopped shallots
  or yellow onion
¼ cup mayonnaise

1 tablespoon prepared horseradish
½ teaspoon salt
1 tablespoon finely chopped green
  onion
Crackers

Heat butter in medium skillet over medium heat. Add liver and shallots and sauté until browned and cooked through.

Grind liver and onion mixture in food grinder or processor until fine. Combine with mayonnaise, horseradish, and salt and transfer to a small serving bowl. Sprinkle with green onion, cover and refrigerate until ready to serve. Serve with crackers.

4 Servings

"This party is great fun if you don't include slackers. The hostess plans an informal dinner party for 12 to cost about $6.00 which is, if you share, 50 cents a head. Menu so planned that guests share the preparation, serving and clean-up job."—*Woman's Home Companion*, November 1942

BRISKET WITH VEGETABLES

★ ★

Perfect for informal entertaining, this one-pot meal watches itself while the cook has time for other things. The abundance of vegetables extends the low-points roast to make it a hearty autumn meal.

1 tablespoon vegetable oil
1 cup coarsely chopped onions
2½ pounds beef brisket
2 cups water
¾ teaspoon salt

¼ teaspoon ground black pepper
6 medium sweet potatoes, peeled and halved crosswise
1 medium head cabbage, cut into 6 wedges

Heat oil in 5-quart Dutch oven over medium heat. Add onions and sauté until golden. Remove onions with a slotted spoon to a bowl.

Add brisket to Dutch oven and brown on all sides. Return onions and any drippings from bowl to Dutch oven. Add water, ½ teaspoon salt, and the pepper.

Cover Dutch oven and simmer 1 to 1½ hours or until brisket is almost tender adding water occasionally, if necessary. Add sweet potatoes and cook 20 minutes. Add cabbage and remaining ¼ teaspoon salt; cook until meat and vegetables reach desired doneness, 10 to 15 minutes longer.

To serve, transfer brisket to serving platter, slice crosswise. Add sweet potatoes and cabbage to platter. Skim off any fat from broth in Dutch oven. Transfer broth and onions to gravy boat and serve with brisket and vegetables. If desired, broth and onions may be puréed in blender.

6 Servings

GIANT CHEESE "HOT DOGS"

★ ★

Hot dogs were often suggested for party fare during the war. This idea from a May 1942 beer advertisement was so cleverly promoted that I just couldn't resist including it. Here's what they promised: "After the card game, you'll be the 'toast of the stag line' when you trump their hearts with this snack. Quick, easy, thrifty . . . an irresistible blend of manly fare and foaming Pabst Blue Ribbon."

8 extra-large frankfurters	**8 strips bacon**
4 slices American cheese	**8 hot dog rolls, toasted**

Preheat broiler. Slit hot dogs lengthwise; cut each cheese slice into 4 strips; place 2 in each hot dog. Wrap bacon tightly around hot dogs and place on broiler pan with slit down.

Broil, turning hot dogs until bacon is well done on all sides. Serve in toasted rolls.

8 Servings

> "As if rationing could change us into Scrooges! Why, it's a dare to start us off on new adventures. This year when love and friendship have taken on a deeper meaning is the time of all times to light the Christmas candles and open wide our hearts and homes."—*Woman's Home Companion*, December 1943

WARTIME SPECIAL

Brunswick Stew

2 pounds boneless veal
   shoulder, cut into strips
2 tablespoons fat
½ teaspoon salt
1 can lima beans

1 can corn
12-ounce can tomato juice
1 teaspoon Worcestershire
   sauce
3 tablespoons flour

Brown veal in fat in a large skillet. Add salt and liquid from canned lima beans and corn. Cover and simmer until meat is tender. Combine tomato juice, Worcestershire sauce, and flour until smooth. Stir into skillet and cook until thickened. Stir in limas and corn. Cook 10 minutes longer.

Serves 6

"One Thanksgiving our meal was highlighted with a make believe turkey made from meat loaf (meat purchased by saving our ration stamps). Legs of the 'turkey' were made by shaping meat loaf around clothes pins and sticking them into the meat loaf."—*Judson H. Stout, Jacksonville Beach, Florida*

HUNGARIAN GOULASH

★ ★

This flavorful stew could be made with small amounts of the less tender cuts of beef, which required fewer ration points. Magazine articles often recommended this as a dish that could be made after dinner one evening and refrigerated to reheat for a small dinner party the next night.

2 tablespoons vegetable oil

3 cups sliced onions

1½ pounds beef chuck or round cut into 1-inch cubes

1 pint home-canned or 1 (15-ounce) can tomatoes

2 tablespoons paprika

1 teaspoon salt

¼ cup water

2 tablespoons flour

Cooked buttered noodles or boiled potatoes

Heat 1 tablespoon oil over medium heat in 5-quart Dutch oven. Add onions and sauté until golden. Remove onions to a bowl.

Heat remaining tablespoon oil in same Dutch oven and brown beef cubes on all sides.

Stir in tomatoes, paprika, and salt. Spoon onions and any drippings from bowl over meat. Cover and simmer 1 to 1½ hours or until beef is tender, adding water if necessary. If desired, cool to room temperature and refrigerate overnight.

To serve, skim off any fat from top of broth. Stir water into flour until smooth; stir into goulash. Bring mixture to a boil over medium heat, stirring occasionally. Serve with buttered noodles or potatoes.

4 Servings

"The army will take about 30% of the cranberry crop this year. Included in that will be all that are dehydrated. Civilians will get the little that is canned."—*American Cookery*, November 1943

INDIVIDUAL LAMB ROASTS

At a time when meat was scarce, a bountiful platter of these roasted lamb shanks, one for each person, must have been an impressive sight for dinner party guests.

¼ cup unsifted all-purpose flour
¾ teaspoon salt
¼ teaspoon ground black pepper
4 cloves garlic, sliced

6 small lamb shanks (4½ pounds)
2 tablespoons vegetable oil
2 cups sliced onions
2 cups water

Combine flour, salt, and pepper in a pie plate. Insert several slices of garlic into each lamb shank. Roll shanks in flour mixture to coat completely. Reserve any remaining flour mixture.

Heat half of oil over medium heat in a 6-quart Dutch oven. Add lamb shanks, several at a time, and brown on all sides; remove to a bowl when browned. When all lamb shanks have been browned, add onions and remaining oil to Dutch oven and sauté until golden. Stir in any reserved flour mixture.

Return lamb shanks and any drippings from bowl to Dutch oven. Add water to Dutch oven. Bring to a boil over high heat. Cover, reduce heat to low, and cook 1½ to 2 hours or until lamb is tender, adding water if necessary.

To serve, transfer lamb shanks to a serving platter. Remove any fat from gravy, add water, if necessary, to thin gravy to pouring consistency. Bring gravy to a boil; pour into a gravy boat and serve with lamb shanks.

6 Servings

JAVANESE CORN WITH COCONUT

★ ★

The addition of a toasted coconut topping turns a bowl of corn into a festive party dish and inspires its exotic name. If using home-canned corn remember that all home-canned nonacid vegetables must be boiled 15 minutes before using.

2 cups fresh corn or 1 pint home-
    canned corn, boiled 15 minutes
    and drained
½ cup cream

⅛ teaspoon salt
⅛ teaspoon ground black pepper
¾ cup grated coconut

Preheat oven to 400°F. Grease a 3- to 4-cup baking dish.

Bring corn, cream, salt, and pepper to a boil in a 1-quart saucepan over medium heat. Pour mixture into greased baking dish and top with coconut.

Bake just until the coconut is golden brown, 10 to 12 minutes.

4 Servings

"Everywhere hostesses are simplifying refreshments. Some ideas gleaned from our readers: Bread, fresh from the oven, sliced and buttered, with hot fragrant tea. A huge bowl of fruit and popcorn balls. Brownies and milk. Crackers, cheese, coffee. Corn on the cob, all the butter you want, coffee. Fish chowder, pilot biscuits, hot gingerbread. Broiled hamburgers in hot rolls, cole slaw, coffee."—*Woman's Home Companion*, May 1942

OAT STICKS

★ ★

These crunchy little sticks are perfect for a buffet because they do not require a knife or butter.

⅔ cup milk

½ cup old-fashioned rolled oats

1¼ cups unsifted all-purpose flour

1 tablespoon light brown sugar

2 teaspoons baking powder

¾ teaspoon salt

¼ cup vegetable shortening or butter
 (or a mixture)

1 large egg, lightly beaten

Heat oven to 400°F. Grease 2 large baking sheets. Warm milk over medium heat in a small saucepan until bubbles appear at the side of the pan. Pour hot milk over rolled oats in a small bowl and set aside 10 minutes.

Meanwhile, combine flour, brown sugar, baking powder, and salt in a medium bowl. Cut shortening into dry ingredients with a pastry blender or 2 knives.

Make a well in the center of dry ingredients. Add milk and oatmeal mixture and stir until mixture forms a ball. Divide dough into 24 equal balls. Roll each with hands to make a 4-inch stick; place 1 inch apart on greased baking sheets. Brush with beaten egg.

Bake oatsticks 12 to 15 minutes or until lightly browned. Cool on pan 5 minutes.

24 Oat Sticks

POTATO CLOVERLEAF ROLLS

★ ★

The idea of substituting mashed potatoes for part of the flour in yeast breads was an old one by the 1940s, but it was right in line with the government's antiwaste campaign. A cup of mashed potatoes that would otherwise be thrown away adds moistness to these honey-sweetened dinner rolls.

⅔ cup milk

1 cup mashed potatoes

¼ cup honey

3 tablespoons vegetable shortening or
   butter (or a mixture)

¾ teaspoon salt

¼ cup warm (105° to 110°F) water

1 package active dry yeast

3½ to 4½ cups unsifted all-purpose
   flour

1 large egg, lightly beaten

Heat milk in a small saucepan over medium heat until bubbles form at edge of pan; stir in mashed potatoes, honey, shortening, and salt. Transfer to a large bowl and set aside to cool to 105° to 110°F.

Combine warm water and yeast in a cup and set aside for yeast to soften.

When milk mixture has cooled, add 3½ cups flour, the beaten egg, and yeast mixture; stir until a soft dough forms. Turn dough out onto a work surface floured with some of remaining 1 cup flour. Knead 5 minutes adding as much flour as necessary to make dough manageable. Place dough in a greased bowl, cover, and set aside in a warm place until double in size—about 1 hour.

Grease a 12-cup muffin pan. Divide dough into 36 equal pieces. Shape each piece into a ball; place 3 balls into each greased cup. Set aside in a warm place until double in size, about 45 minutes.

Preheat oven to 400°F. Bake rolls 20 to 25 minutes, or until golden brown and a roll sounds hollow when tapped on top. Cool at least 15 minutes before serving.

12 Servings

RAISED CHOCOLATE CAKE

★ ★

This unusual cake rises to impressive heights because of the yeast in the recipe. I had made it several times in the 1960s and forgotten about it until I started to see the recipe in wartime magazines and cookbooks.

¾ cup warm water (105° to 110°F)
1 envelope active dry yeast
⅔ cup packed light brown sugar
½ cup shortening
2 large eggs
½ cup light corn syrup
1 teaspoon vanilla extract

2 cups sifted cake flour (sift before measuring)
⅓ cup unsweetened cocoa
½ teaspoon baking soda
½ teaspoon salt
Sugarless Boiled Frosting, optional, recipe page 97

Grease two deep 8-inch round baking pans. Combine warm water and yeast in a cup and set aside for yeast to soften.

Beat together brown sugar and shortening until fluffy. Beat in eggs one at a time, then corn syrup and vanilla.

Stir together flour, cocoa, baking soda, and salt. Add to sugar mixture along with yeast mixture. Beat just until smooth.

Divide batter between greased pans and set aside in a warm place 30 minutes or until it begins to look puffy.

Preheat oven to 350°F. Bake layers 25 to 30 minutes or until a toothpick inserted in center of each comes out clean. Remove to wire racks to cool completely before frosting. Fill and frost with Sugarless Boiled Frosting, if desired.

12 Servings

WARTIME SPECIAL

Mint Tinkle

1¼ cups warm water
¾ cup white corn syrup
½ cup lemon juice
½ teaspoon mint extract

Several drops green food
   coloring
1 (24-ounce) bottle ginger ale
Crushed ice

Combine water, corn syrup, lemon juice, mint extract, and food coloring; chill until ready to serve. To serve, combine with ginger ale and ice.

6 Servings

"I was a very new bride in 1943 and because my husband was overseas did not do much cooking. . . . I do remember the rationing and the struggle to find meat, sugar, etc. When I married, we had to provide the sugar for the wedding cake to the baker."—*Natalie M. Quinn, Pennock, Minnesota*

CHOCOLATE SPANISH CREAM

Spanish Cream appeared in a variety of flavors on 1940s' menus. It was a little easier to make in those days (before the concern about raw egg safety) by just separating the eggs and folding the beaten whites in at the end. However, today we can still re-create this fluffy dessert using meringue powder or sterilized egg white powder.

3 cups milk

1 envelope unflavored gelatin

1 cup light corn syrup

2 ounces unsweetened chocolate, chopped

¼ teaspoon salt

2 large eggs

2 teaspoons vanilla extract

3 tablespoons meringue powder, see Note

⅓ cup water

Combine milk and gelatin in top of double boiler; set aside 5 minutes to soften. Add corn syrup, chocolate, and salt; place over hot but not boiling water, and heat gently until gelatin and chocolate have melted.

Meanwhile, beat eggs until thick and lemon-colored. Gradually beat in half of milk mixture. Return to milk mixture in double boiler and cook, stirring, just until mixture thickens. Pour into a medium bowl, stir in vanilla, and set aside, stirring occasionally, until slightly cooled, no longer than 30 minutes.

Whip meringue powder and water together until soft peaks form. Fold meringue mixture into chocolate mixture until no white streaks show. Transfer to serving bowl, cover and refrigerate until firm, about 3 to 4 hours.

6 Servings

NOTE: Or, follow package directions to use sterilized egg white powder plus water equivalent to 3 egg whites.

STRAWBERRY OR RASPBERRY TRIFLE

★ ★

A layer of the Sugarless Two-Egg Cake (see page 94) is perfect here because it isn't too sweet, but you could use a commercial sponge cake layer or even a frozen pound cake.

2 cups heavy cream

1 teaspoon sugar

1 teaspoon vanilla extract

1 (8-inch) plain cake layer

1 cup strawberry or raspberry jam or
  preserves

¼ cup ruby port

½ cup slivered blanched almonds

1 cup fresh strawberries or
  raspberries, optional

Whip cream with sugar and vanilla until stiff peaks form. Cut cake into ¼-inch-thick slices; halve center slices so that all are 3 to 4 inches long. Stir together jam and port.

Spoon about ¾ cup whipped cream into bottom of a 2-quart glass bowl or soufflé dish. Top with one third of cake slices and about ⅓ cup of jam mixture. Repeat twice ending with all remaining whipped cream.

Cover trifle and refrigerate at least 4 hours before serving.

Meanwhile, toast almonds in a heavy skillet over medium heat, shaking frequently until golden. Immediately pour into small bowl to stop browning; set aside. If using berries, rinse, drain well, and refrigerate until ready to serve.

To serve, sprinkle almonds over top and garnish with berries, if desired.

8 Servings

FLAKY PASTRY

★ ★

Single-crust pies were encouraged during the war because they used half as much shortening as a standard pie. Except for holidays, when an occasional double-crust pie recipe appeared, most dessert articles advised that "you don't have to give up pie, just give up the top crust." This "low-shortening" crust makes two single-crust pies or a double-crust one.

2¼ cups unsifted all-purpose flour
½ teaspoon salt

½ cup lard or vegetable shortening
4 to 5 tablespoons ice water

Preheat oven to 375°F. Combine flour and salt in a medium bowl. Cut in lard or shortening with a pastry blender or 2 knives until crumbs are size of a small pea.

Gradually add water, stirring with a fork just until mixture will form a ball. The less water used the better. Divide dough in half.

Roll out 1 ball of dough to an 11-inch round. Transfer to a 9-inch pie plate; turn under and flute edges. Pierce the bottom ten to twelve times with the tines of a fork. Repeat with remaining dough. Wrap and refrigerate for up to 5 days, or bake until golden, about 15 minutes—and fill, or cool, wrap, and store in a tin at room temperature for up to 1 week.

2 (9-inch) Pastry Shells

"Some things you'll be missing on this Thanksgiving table. No oysters, no plum pudding, no 'boiled-cider applesass.' The mincemeat didn't get a play this time, but there's plenty just the same, and every single dish *belongs.*"—*Ladies' Home Journal,* November 1944

CARROT PIE

★ ★

Although there was no shortage of pumpkins, commercially canned pumpkin was rationed and was difficult to get because it was in demand by service commissaries. With the proper seasoning, fresh or home-canned carrots from the Victory Garden produced a delicious alternative for the duration.

2 cups pureed cooked carrots	1 teaspoon vanilla extract
½ cup packed light brown sugar	½ teaspoon ground nutmeg
½ cup milk	½ teaspoon salt
3 large eggs, lightly beaten	¼ teaspoon ground cloves
2 tablespoons all-purpose flour	1 (9-inch) unbaked pastry shell
1 teaspoon ground cinnamon	Sweetened whipped cream, optional

Preheat oven to 350°F.

Thoroughly combine carrots, brown sugar, milk, eggs, flour, cinnamon, vanilla, nutmeg, salt, and cloves in a large bowl. Transfer mixture to pastry shell; smooth top surface.

Bake pie until center looks set when pie is gently tapped, 45 to 50 minutes. Cool to room temperature, then chill several hours before serving. Just before serving, top with whipped cream, if desired.

8 Servings

"Ready For Thanksgiving . . . Patriotic War Stamp corsages for the ladies and boutonnieres for the men await the guests."—*Good Housekeeping*, November 1943

RHUBARB PIE

★ ★

One of the first signs of spring in the garden, rhubarb makes a fitting celebration pie for Easter. Not usually something you would think of cooking when sugar is scarce, tangy rhubarb is deliciously tamed with the use of raspberry jam.

2 pounds rhubarb, cut into 1-inch
    pieces (about 6 cups)
1¼ cups seedless red raspberry
    preserves, melted

¼ cup cornstarch
¼ teaspoon salt
1 recipe Flaky Pastry (page 211)

Preheat oven to 375°F.

Combine rhubarb, preserves, cornstarch, and salt in a large bowl, making sure that cornstarch is evenly distributed.

Roll out half of dough to an 11-inch round. Transfer to a 9-inch pie plate; fill with rhubarb mixture. Moisten edge of pastry. Roll out remaining half of dough to a 10-inch round. Cut a hole in center and place over filling. Turn excess pastry under and flute edges. Place pie on rimmed baking sheet.

Bake pie until crust is golden and filling bubbles through center hole, about 45 minutes. Cool to room temperature on wire rack before cutting.

8 Servings

CHOCOLATE MARSHMALLOW PIE

★ ★

Entertaining articles often suggested that couples invite their friends over for dessert. This elegant marshmallow-sweetened pie would be perfect for just such an occasion. And if you offer a cup of coffee with it, the evening would get four stars.

24 marshmallows
½ cup milk
2 ounces unsweetened chocolate,
  chopped

¾ cup heavy cream
2 tablespoons confectioners' sugar
¼ teaspoon almond extract
1 (8-inch) graham cracker pie shell

Heat marshmallows, milk, and chocolate in the top of a double boiler, over hot, but not boiling, water, stirring constantly just until marshmallows and chocolate have melted and mixture is smooth. Pour into a medium bowl; cover and refrigerate until completely cool, stirring occasionally.

Meanwhile, whip cream, confectioners' sugar, and almond extract until stiff peaks form. When marshmallow mixture is cool, fold cream into it.

Spoon mixture into graham cracker pie shell, swirling filling in center. Refrigerate at least 4 hours before serving.

8 Servings

"No need to spend your holiday in the kitchen while everyone else is having fun! With proper planning and the help of your refrigerator you can avoid the last-minute rush and fuss of holiday preparation. Practically your entire dinner can be prepared in advance and stored in your refrigerator, ready for the range."—*Frigidaire advertisement, 1943*

10

PINK SLIPS LEAD TO PINK APRONS

★ ★ ★ ★ ★ ★ ★ ★ ★ ★ ★ ★ ★ ★ ★ ★ ★ ★ ★ ★

Chicken à la King

Beef Stroganoff

Rib Roast with Mushroom Gravy

Stuffed Cabbage Leaves

Swiss Steak

Spaghetti and Meatballs

Macaroni and Cheese

Scalloped Potatoes

Hot Potato Salad

Refrigerator Sticky Buns

Icebox Cookies

Apple Dumplings

Strawberry Shortcake

Ribbon Cake

Zebra Cake

As the war ended, women's jobs disappeared. Many women would have liked to continue working, but massive layoffs started the day after Japan surrendered. Working-class women had to return to low-paying jobs to contribute to the support of their families, and middle-class women had few choices other than to return to the kitchen. At first supplies were even more scarce than they had been during the war. Much American food was sent to Europe where for five years the land had been neglected or destroyed. This was a time of transition. Some wartime recipes still provided comfort at a time when women were redefining their lives. There was money to buy steak and new kitchen appliances just as soon as the nation could convert to peacetime production. And soon there were supermarkets and all those new convenience foods. This chapter focuses on the dishes that emerged from the war as "keepers"—those that became a part of the mainstream American menu even when we could buy anything we wanted.

In this brief period between Victory Gardens and TV dinners women rechanneled their energies into the home and confirmed that they had not left the kitchen—at least not yet. Meat- and butter-rich meals replaced vegetable main dishes and steak on the grill was the height of entertaining. Herbs languished on the back shelf and the sugar bowl returned to its prewar spot on the family dining table. Yet GIs brought home the memory of the ethnic dishes they had tasted "over there" and America would soon experiment with French, Italian, and Chinese dishes.

CHICKEN À LA KING

This dish made an elegant ladies' luncheon or a not-too-hearty summer supper. The recipe later came to be made with canned cream of chicken, mushroom, or celery soup.

3 tablespoons butter

¼ cup unsifted all-purpose flour

½ teaspoon salt

⅛ teaspoon ground black pepper

2 cups milk

2 cups cooked boneless chicken pieces

½ cup frozen green peas

3 tablespoons chopped pimiento

4 baked puff pastry patty shells

Melt butter in a heavy saucepan over low heat. Stir in flour, salt, and pepper until smooth. Very gradually stir in milk; cook over low heat, stirring constantly until sauce has thickened.

Fold chicken, peas, and pimiento into sauce and cook over low heat until everything is heated through, 5 to 10 minutes.

To serve, place patty shells on 4 dinner plates. Spoon chicken mixture into and around patty shells; serve immediately.

4 Servings

"In 1944, those groups which had welcomed, even urged, women to take jobs began to roll up the welcome mat. . . . While public spokesmen of all sorts proposed a variety of means to ensure full employment, they all assumed that a partial solution was the retirement of millions of women to domesticity."—*The Homefront and Beyond*, 1982

BEEF STROGANOFF

★ ★

This recipe had all the elements necessary for a sophisticated postwar party dish—lots of beef and cream, and an international heritage.

2 tablespoons butter

1¼ pounds boneless sirloin steak, cut
   into ½- by 2-inch strips

1½ cups thinly sliced mushrooms

¼ cup finely chopped onion

1 clove garlic, finely chopped

3 tablespoons all-purpose flour

1 tablespoon tomato paste, optional

¼ to ½ teaspoon salt

¼ teaspoon ground black pepper

¾ cup beef broth

1 cup dairy sour cream

3 cups hot cooked white and wild
   rice

Melt butter over medium heat in a 4-quart Dutch oven. Add sirloin and sauté until well browned on all sides. Remove to a bowl.

Add mushrooms, onion, and garlic to drippings in Dutch oven and sauté until browned. Stir flour, tomato paste, if using, ¼ teaspoon salt, and the pepper into mushroom mixture. Gradually add broth and cook, stirring constantly until thickened. Reduce heat to low and cook 5 minutes.

Return beef and any drippings in bowl to Dutch oven. Fold in sour cream; heat just until mixture is very hot but not boiling. Taste and add salt, if necessary. Serve with white and wild rice.

4 Servings

RIB ROAST WITH MUSHROOM GRAVY

★ ★

Once beef was back, this elegant roast became a classic special-occasion meal. The roast so dominated the meal that it was often simply accompanied by baked potatoes, salad, and a vegetable.

1 (5-pound) beef standing rib roast
½ to ¾ teaspoon salt
¼ teaspoon ground black pepper
1 cup boiling water

1 tablespoon butter
3 cups sliced mushrooms
½ cup dry red wine
¼ cup all-purpose flour

Preheat oven to 325°F. Place roast in a shallow roasting pan. Sprinkle with ¼ teaspoon salt and pepper. Place in center of oven and roast 2¼ to 2¾ hours or until a meat thermometer inserted in center of roast registers 150°F for medium-rare or 160°F for medium. Remove to platter and let stand 15 minutes before carving.

Pour drippings from pan into a 1-quart measuring cup. Add boiling water to pan and stir to remove browned-on bits; add pan liquid to drippings in cup; remove fat from drippings mixture.

Melt butter in a large skillet over medium heat; sauté mushrooms until golden. Pour off mushroom liquid into measuring cup with drippings. Add cold water, if necessary, to make 3 cups; return mixture to skillet with mushrooms. Stir wine into flour until smooth. Add to mushroom mixture along with another ¼ teaspoon of salt and cook, stirring constantly until sauce boils and thickens. Taste and add more salt, if necessary. Serve with rib roast.

8 Servings

STUFFED CABBAGE LEAVES

★ ★

The filling for these savory rolls is often made with uncooked ground beef or pork and cooked for up to 1 hour. However, using leftover meat makes the recipe thrifty, and saves cooking time.

1 cup water

8 large green cabbage leaves

1 teaspoon bacon fat or vegetable shortening

½ cup finely chopped onion

½ cup chopped green bell pepper

1½ cups cooked rice

1 cup chopped cooked meat (use leftover beef, pork, chicken, or a mix)

¼ teaspoon salt, optional

⅛ to ¼ teaspoon cayenne pepper

1 cup tomato juice

2 tablespoons cider vinegar

1 tablespoon sugar

2 tablespoons all-purpose flour

Bring ¾ cup water to a boil in a 4-quart Dutch oven. Add cabbage leaves; cover and remove from heat; set aside 5 minutes.

Meanwhile, heat bacon fat over medium heat in a small skillet. Add onion and green pepper and sauté until lightly browned. Stir in rice, meat, salt, if needed, and desired amount of red pepper. Moisten with 2 tablespoons hot cooking liquid from Dutch oven.

Remove cabbage leaves to a colander, reserving cooking liquid in Dutch oven. Drain leaves well and arrange on a flat surface; flatten any large ribs with blade of a knife. Divide meat mixture onto cabbage leaves. Turn sides of leaves over filling and roll up to completely enclose filling. Fasten with toothpick.

Stir tomato juice, vinegar, and sugar into reserved cooking liquid in Dutch oven. Place cabbage rolls into tomato juice mixture in Dutch oven in a single layer. Cover and bring to a boil; simmer 15 minutes.

To serve, remove cabbage rolls to platter; keep warm. Stir flour into remaining ¼ cup water and stir into tomato juice mixture. Bring mixture to a boil over medium heat, stirring until thickened. Spoon some tomato sauce over cabbage rolls; transfer remaining sauce to a small pitcher and serve with cabbage rolls.

4 Servings

SWISS STEAK

★ ★

I was surprised to find small amounts of curry powder used for seasoning in many recipes that no longer call for it. Along with paprika and celery salt, it seems to have been a staple in the 1940s spice cupboard.

2 tablespoons all-purpose flour

½ teaspoon curry powder

¼ teaspoon salt

1 pound round steak

1½ tablespoons vegetable shortening or butter (or a mixture)

1 cup diced carrots

1 cup coarsely chopped string beans

3 tablespoons chopped green bell pepper

1 tablespoon chopped onion

1 pint home-canned or 1 (15-ounce) can tomatoes

Combine flour, curry powder, and salt in a pie plate. Cut steak into 4 pieces. Coat pieces completely in flour mixture; reserve any remaining flour mixture.

Melt half of shortening in a large heavy skillet over medium heat. Brown meat well on one side. Turn meat and brown other side in remaining shortening. Sprinkle any remaining flour mixture around meat.

Spoon carrots, beans, pepper, and onion over steaks. Pour tomatoes over all. Cover and simmer until meat is tender, about 1 hour, adding water if needed to keep meat from scorching.

To serve, remove meat to warm serving platter. Remove and discard any fat from vegetable mixture; stir mixture and spoon over steaks. If vegetable mixture is too thin, cook, uncovered, stirring constantly until it reaches desired consistency before spooning over steaks.

4 Servings

WARTIME SPECIAL

Angel Food Fruit Ring

1 can fruit cocktail

1 tablespoon lemon juice

1 package unflavored gelatin

2 cups cubed angel food cake

1 ice cube

Drain fruit cocktail, reserving the syrup. Cover and refrigerate the fruit. Combine ¼ cup of the syrup from the fruit with the lemon juice and gelatin in a custard cup; set aside 5 minutes for the gelatin to soften. Combine the remaining fruit syrup and the ice cube in a large bowl. Place the cup of gelatin mixture in a pan of boiling water set off the heat and stir until the gelatin dissolves. Add to the syrup in the large bowl and stir until the ice cube melts. Fold in the angel food cake squares and pack into a well-oiled 4-cup ring mold. Chill until firm. Unmold onto a serving platter and fill with the chilled fruit cocktail.

4 Servings

SPAGHETTI AND MEATBALLS

★ ★

Everybody looked forward to spaghetti night. It took a while for American cooks to learn how to make Italian tomato sauce, but they gradually got better and better at it. I can't pretend that this sauce is Italian, but it is a step closer than the kind we made during the war years.

1 pound ground beef	½ cup chopped onion
1 egg	2 (14½-ounce) cans stewed tomatoes
¼ cup Italian seasoned dry bread crumbs	1 (8-ounce) can tomato sauce
2 cloves garlic, finely chopped	1 teaspoon dried basil leaves
½ teaspoon salt, plus more for cooking spaghetti	½ teaspoon dried oregano leaves
	1 (8-ounce) package spaghetti
1 tablespoon olive or vegetable oil	Grated Parmesan cheese, optional

Combine ground beef, egg, bread crumbs, half of garlic, and ¼ teaspoon salt in a small bowl. Shape into 12 meatballs. Heat oil over medium heat in a large heavy saucepan. Add meatballs and sauté until brown on all sides. Push to one side and add onion and remaining garlic; sauté until onion is golden.

Stir stewed tomatoes, tomato sauce, basil, oregano, and remaining ¼ teaspoon salt into meatball mixture. Bring to a boil over low heat; cover and simmer 20 minutes.

Meanwhile, cook spaghetti according to package directions. Drain well and divide onto 4 plates. Top with meatballs and sauce and serve with cheese, if desired.

4 to 6 Servings

MACARONI AND CHEESE

★ ★

A meatless main dish that everyone in the family loves, this convenient casserole extended rationed ingredients with lots of pasta. When the war ended, American homemakers kept right on making it and although still a relatively inexpensive way to provide protein, no one thinks of Macaroni and Cheese as anything other than a delicious and comforting main dish.

1 (8-ounce) package macaroni

3 tablespoons vegetable shortening or
　butter (or a mixture)

3 tablespoons unsifted all-purpose
　flour

½ teaspoon dry mustard

¼ to ½ teaspoon salt

2½ cups milk

1½ cups grated Cheddar cheese

1¼ cups day-old whole-wheat or
　white bread crumbs (from 3 to
　4 slices bread)

1 tablespoon butter, melted

Cook macaroni according to package directions. Drain well.

Meanwhile, melt shortening in a heavy saucepan over low heat. Remove from heat; stir in flour, mustard, and ¼ to ½ teaspoon salt until smooth. Very gradually stir in milk. Cook over low heat, stirring constantly until sauce has thickened. Fold in ½ cup cheese.

Preheat oven to 350°F. Generously grease a 9-inch (6-cup) baking dish. Place one third of macaroni in dish in an even layer. Top with ½ cup cheese sauce and ¼ cup cheese; repeat once. Top with remaining macaroni, sauce, and cheese. Combine crumbs and butter. Sprinkle evenly over top. Place on rimmed baking sheet and bake 30 to 35 minutes or until browned and bubbly.

4 to 6 Servings

SCALLOPED POTATOES

★ ★

Just add a little bit of ham or bacon to make this favorite side dish a hearty meal.

1½ pounds all-purpose potatoes,
   peeled and thinly sliced
2 tablespoons vegetable shortening or
   bacon fat
3 tablespoons flour

½ teaspoon salt
½ teaspoon dry mustard
2 cups milk
2 large onions, thinly sliced
Cooked bacon or ham, optional

Cook potatoes in boiling salted water to cover 10 minutes. Drain well.

Meanwhile, in a heavy saucepan, over low heat, melt shortening. Stir in flour, salt, and mustard until smooth. Very gradually stir in milk; cook over low heat, stirring constantly until sauce has thickened.

Preheat oven to 350°F. Generously grease a 9-inch (6-cup) baking dish. Place one third of potatoes in dish in an even layer; top with one third of onions and ½ cup sauce. Repeat layering twice, ending with 1 cup sauce. If desired, add bacon or ham with onions in first 2 layers.

Place on rimmed baking sheet and bake 40 to 45 minutes or until browned and bubbly.

6 Servings

> "When after the war, the abundance can be had again—even greater than before the war—the American people will be able to resume their climb up the ladder of better living standards."—*Battle Stations for All*, 1943

HOT POTATO SALAD

★ ★

A mid-war magazine article reminded cooks that there were plenty of potatoes and offered a variety of ways to turn them into main dishes. This savory dish was one and easily made the transition to the 1950s kitchen. It can be used as an accompaniment or, with the addition of some leftover ham, as a main dish. It can even be made with leftover cooked potatoes; just skip the first step.

1 pound potatoes, cut into ¾-inch cubes (4 cups)

4 slices bacon

½ cup chopped onion

½ cup chopped green bell pepper

1 tablespoon flour

½ cup water

2 tablespoons cider vinegar

1 teaspoon sugar

¼ to ½ teaspoon salt

⅛ teaspoon ground black pepper

1 large egg

Bring potatoes and salted water to cover to a boil in a 3-quart saucepan over high heat. Reduce heat to low and simmer, covered, 15 minutes or until just tender. Drain and set aside in saucepan.

Meanwhile, fry bacon in a medium skillet over medium heat until crisp and brown. Remove and drain, reserving bacon fat in pan. Add onion and bell pepper to skillet and sauté until they start to brown. Stir in flour. Gradually stir in water, vinegar, sugar, ¼ teaspoon salt, and the black pepper. Cook 1 minute.

Lightly beat egg in a small bowl. Very gradually beat some of hot vinegar mixture into egg, then return mixture to the skillet and bring just to a boil, stirring constantly. Pour over potatoes and stir to coat potatoes well. Taste and add more salt if necessary. Transfer to a serving bowl. Crumble bacon over top.

4 Servings

REFRIGERATOR STICKY BUNS

★ ★

This recipe was a treasure to war workers used to pleasing their family with homemade yeast breads. The buns could be prepared—ready for their last rising and refrigerated—while the cook went off to work. When she returned 10 hours later, they were ready to bake and serve. Without the cinnamon filling and sticky topping, the dough could also be made into a dozen different shapes of dinner rolls. We have continued to make them to this day.

Roll Dough:

⅔ cup milk

⅓ cup vegetable shortening or
    butter (or a mixture)

2 tablespoons light brown sugar

½ teaspoon salt

¼ cup warm (105° to 110°F) water

1 package active dry yeast

1 large egg, lightly beaten

3½ to 4 cups unsifted all-purpose flour

Filling and Topping:

1 tablespoon butter, softened

1 tablespoon granulated sugar

½ teaspoon ground cinnamon

1 cup light corn syrup

¼ cup packed light brown sugar

1 cup pecan halves

Prepare roll dough: Heat milk in a small saucepan over medium heat until bubbles form at edge of pan; stir in shortening, brown sugar, and salt. Pour mixture into a large bowl; set aside to cool to between 105° and 110°F.

Meanwhile, combine warm water and yeast in a cup and set aside for yeast to soften.

When milk mixture has cooled, beat in egg and yeast mixture. Add 3½ cups flour and stir until a soft dough forms.

Turn dough out onto a work surface floured with some of remaining ½ cup flour. Knead 5 minutes adding as much of remaining flour as necessary to make dough manageable. Place dough in a greased bowl, cover, and set aside in a warm place until double in size, about 1 hour.

Fill and shape buns: Grease a 13- by 9-inch glass baking dish. Roll out dough to a 16- by 12-inch rectangle. Spread with softened butter and sprinkle with granulated sugar and cinnamon. Roll up to make a 16-inch log. Cut crosswise into 16 pieces. Combine syrup and brown sugar in bottom of baking dish; sprinkle pecans over mixture. Place buns with a cut side up in baking dish. Cover loosely and refrigerate 8 to 10 hours.

Unwrap buns and place in cold oven. Turn on oven to 350°F. Bake 25 to 30 minutes or until golden brown and buns sound hollow when tapped on top. Loosen buns from edges of baking dish and invert onto a serving tray immediately. Cool at least 30 minutes before serving.

16 Servings

WARTIME SPECIAL

Fisherman's Loaf

1 (1-pound) loaf unsliced
   firm white bread
1 tablespoon butter, softened
1 can peas
2 tablespoons vegetable
   shortening

2 tablespoons all-purpose
   flour
¼ teaspoon salt
¼ cup heavy cream
1 cup cooked or canned
   shrimp

Trim crusts from bread; remove center of loaf leaving a ½-inch shell. Brush surfaces of bread with butter; bake at 400°F until well browned. Drain peas, reserving ¾ cup liquid. Heat shortening in a saucepan; stir in flour and salt. Gradually stir in reserved liquid from peas and the cream. Cook, stirring until thickened. Add peas and shrimp; cook 2 minutes. Spoon into bread case.

ICEBOX COOKIES

★ ★

Although we got our first refrigerator well before the 1940s, we still call these icebox cookies. They are the ultimate quick trick for busy days and postwar homemakers continued to make them. Perhaps that's how they were able to greet the children with a plate of warm cookies as they returned from school. These days, I always have a roll of them in the freezer to slice and bake when I need a quick dessert. Just the aroma of them baking assures the family that the cook is on duty.

1½ cups unsifted all-purpose flour
1 teaspoon baking powder
¼ teaspoon salt
½ cup vegetable shortening or butter
  (or a mixture)

½ cup packed light brown sugar
½ cup granulated sugar
1 large egg, lightly beaten
1 teaspoon vanilla extract

Stir together flour, baking powder, and salt; set aside. Beat together shortening, brown sugar, and granulated sugar in a medium bowl until fluffy. Beat in egg and vanilla.

Shape dough into a roll about 2 inches in diameter; wrap and refrigerate for up to 4 days or freeze for up to 6 months.

When ready to bake, preheat oven to 375°F. Grease 2 baking sheets. Slice dough into ⅛-inch-thick rounds and place 1 inch apart on baking sheets. Bake 8 to 10 minutes or until golden at edges. Cool and serve or pack in an airtight container.

Variation: Divide dough in half. Knead 1 ounce of melted unsweetened chocolate into half of dough. Roll out each dough half to a 12-inch square. Place chocolate square on top of vanilla one and roll up. Chill and bake as above.

48 Cookies

APPLE DUMPLINGS

★ ★

I don't know why the saying isn't "As American as Apple Dumplings." This traditional dessert has weathered many a war and is still a favorite all over the country. In 1946, it was certainly nice to once again have enough sugar and butter to make these as delicious as they could be.

1 recipe Flaky Pastry (page 211)
½ cup sugar
1 teaspoon ground cinnamon
6 medium apples, peeled and
    cored

2 tablespoons butter, cut into 6 equal
    chunks
⅓ cup maple syrup
Cream or sweetened whipped cream,
    optional

Preheat oven to 375°F. Grease a 13- by 9-inch baking pan or dish.

Roll out dough to make an 18- by 12-inch rectangle. Cut dough into 6-inch squares.

Combine sugar and cinnamon in a pie plate. Roll apples, one at a time, in sugar mixture, tuck a chunk of butter into center of each apple, and wrap apple completely in one of pastry squares, pinching edges together. Place in greased pan, pinched edges down. When all are wrapped, pierce a hole in top of each; drizzle maple syrup over them.

Bake dumplings 30 to 35 minutes or until juices start to bubble out of pastry at the bottom. Remove to individual soup plates and serve hot with cream or whipped cream, if desired.

6 Servings

STRAWBERRY SHORTCAKE

★ ★

When the local strawberries arrive, there is no better way to showcase them than in this old-fashioned biscuit shortcake.

2 cups unsifted all-purpose flour

6 tablespoons sugar

4 teaspoons baking powder

¼ teaspoon salt

½ cup butter

⅔ cup milk

1 large egg, beaten

2 teaspoons vanilla extract

4 cups sliced strawberries

1 cup heavy cream

2 tablespoons confectioners' sugar

Preheat oven to 375°F. Lightly grease a large baking sheet.

Combine flour, 3 tablespoons sugar, the baking powder, and salt in a medium bowl. Cut in butter with a pastry blender or 2 knives until mixture forms coarse crumbs.

Combine milk, egg, and 1 teaspoon vanilla. Add to flour mixture and stir together just until all flour mixture has been moistened. Spoon about two thirds of dough onto greased baking sheet to make 6 large biscuits; spoon remaining one third of dough to make 6 small biscuits. Sprinkle 1 tablespoon of the remaining sugar over biscuits. Bake for 15 to 20 minutes or until lightly browned. Cool 15 minutes on baking sheet.

Meanwhile, stir the remaining 2 tablespoons sugar into strawberries. Whip cream with confectioners' sugar and remaining 1 teaspoon vanilla until just stiff; spoon into serving bowl.

To serve, place large biscuits on dessert plates, spoon about two thirds of strawberries over biscuits. Top each with a small biscuit and some of remaining strawberries. Serve with whipped cream.

6 Servings

RIBBON CAKE

★ ★

The recipe for this pretty cake did appear during the war but was a very special occasion cake in those days. Although it uses lots of granulated sugar to celebrate the fact that postwar housewives had as much as they wanted, it had not yet made the transition back to butter.

3 cups sifted cake flour (sift before measuring)

5 teaspoons baking powder

1 teaspoon salt

2 cups sugar

¾ cup vegetable shortening or butter (or a mixture)

3 large egg whites

½ cup milk

1 teaspoon vanilla extract

2 tablespoons unsweetened cocoa

1 tablespoon water

1 teaspoon ground cinnamon

¼ teaspoon ground cloves

3 to 4 drops red food coloring

¼ cup very finely chopped natural almonds

½ teaspoon almond extract

Vanilla-Almond Frosting (recipe follows)

Preheat oven to 350°F. Grease three 8-inch round baking pans. Stir together flour, baking powder, and salt.

Beat together sugar and shortening until fluffy. Beat in egg whites one at a time. Add flour mixture to sugar mixture along with milk and vanilla. Beat just until smooth.

Divide batter into 3 small bowls. Add cocoa, water, cinnamon, and cloves to 1 bowl, red food coloring to another, and almonds and almond extract to third. Spoon each batter into a greased pan.

Bake 25 to 30 minutes or until a toothpick inserted in center of each layer comes out clean. Cool, then fill and frost with Vanilla-Almond Frosting.

VANILLA-ALMOND FROSTING: Beat together 1½ pounds confectioners' sugar, ⅓ cup vegetable shortening, 5 to 6 tablespoons milk, and 1½ teaspoons vanilla and ¾ teaspoon almond extracts until smooth.

4 Servings

ZEBRA CAKE

★ ★

This easy-to-make icebox cake seems to be as popular today as it was 50 years ago. I learned to make it from my grandmother-in-law. Ever since, it has been the favored holiday dessert in our home. For a few years I tried to upstage it with a homemade croquembouche, but everyone said "How pretty" and had a piece of Zebra Cake instead.

1½ cups heavy cream

2 tablespoons confectioners' sugar

2 teaspoons vanilla extract

1 (9-ounce) package chocolate wafer cookies

¼ cup grated chocolate or finely chopped nuts

Beat cream, sugar, and vanilla until stiff peaks form. Spread a generous measuring teaspoon of cream on each cookie. Press cookies together to make 3-inch stacks.

Spread a 1-inch line of whipped cream down center of a serving platter. Assemble cookie stacks into a log on platter. Frost with remaining whipped cream and sprinkle with chocolate or nuts. Cover tightly and refrigerate overnight. To serve, slice diagonally to create striped pieces.

6 Servings

> "One of our greatest treats was the first salad of the season, made with the small wonderful leaf lettuce, chopped green onions, crisp bacon crumbled (when the ration coupons permitted) and boiled sliced eggs, topped with a creamy vinegar dressing. As a side dish, young carrots sautéed in oleo, but still crisp, either malt sugar or brown sugar would be added and simmered until the carrots turned opaque. As the main course—the often appearing macaroni and cheese casserole, baked until lemony brown and bubbly." *Ruth B. Snyder, Chino, California*

Sources

American Meat Institute. *Thriftier Cuts of Meat*. Chicago: AMI, 1941.

Altrista Corporation, Bell Blue Book: Guide to Home Canning, Freezing and Dehydration, 1997.

Anderson, Jean. *The American Century Cookbook*. New York: Clarkson N. Potter, 1997.

Anderson, Karen. *Wartime Women: Sex Roles, Family Relations, and the Status of Women During World War II*. Westport, Conn.: Greenwood Press, 1981.

Arnold-Forster, Mark. *The World at War*. New York: Stein and Day, 1983.

Bentley, Amy Lynn. *Eating for Victory: Food Rationing and the Politics of Domesticity*. Urbana Ill.: University of Illinois Press, 1998.

Better Homes and Gardens Magazine, January 1940 through December 1945.

Blum, John Morton. *V Was for Victory: Politics and American Culture During World War II*. New York: Harcourt Brace Jovanovich, 1976.

Brinkley, David. *Washington Goes to War: The Extraordinary Story of the Transformation of a City and a Nation*. New York: Ballantine Books, 1988.

Brokaw, Tom. *The Greatest Generation*. New York: Random House, 1998.

Campbell, D'Ann. *Women at War with America: Private Lives in a Patriotic Era*. Cambridge, Mass.: Harvard University Press, 1984.

Casdorph, Paul D. *Let the Good Times Roll: Life at Home in America During WWII*. New York: Paragon House, 1991.

Case, Elizabeth, and Martha Wyman. *Cook's Away: A Collection of Simple Rules, Helpful Facts, and Choice Recipes Designed to Make Cooking Easy*. New York: Longmans, Green and Co., 1943.

Crocker, Betty. *Your Share: How to Prepare Appetizing, Healthful Meals with Foods Available Today*. Minneapolis: General Mills, 1943.

Fisher, Ida, ed. *Food as We Like It*. West Springfield, Mass.: Eastern States Farmers' Exchange, 1943.

Frigidaire Corporation. *Wartime Suggestions to Help You Get the Most Out of Your Refrigerator*. Dayton, Ohio: General Motors, 1943.

General Foods Corporation. *Recipes for Today*. White Plains, New York: General Foods Corporation, 1943.

Gifford, Marie. *69 Ration Recipes for Meat from Marie Gifford's Kitchen*. Chicago: Armour and Company, undated.

Gluck, Sherna Berger, ed. *Rosie the Riveter Revisited: Women and the World War II Experience*. Boston: Twayne, 1987.

Good Housekeeping Institute. Easy Ways to Save Sugar: Cooking, Canning, Jelly Making with Little or No Sugar. New York: Hearst Corp., 1942.

Good Housekeeping Magazine. January 1940 through December 1945.

Goodwin, Doris Kearns. *No Ordinary Time: Franklin and Eleanor Roosevelt: The Home Front in World War II.* New York: Touchstone, 1994.

Hackney, Mrs. G. Edgar, comp., Ann R. Silver, ed. *Dining for Moderns.* New York: New York Exchange for Women's Work, 1940.

Hartmann, Susan. *The Homefront and Beyond: American Women in the 1940s.* Boston: Twayne, 1982.

Home Service Bureau, The. *Biscuits and Breads.* Baltimore: The Gas & Electric Company, March 1945.

————. *Home Canning and Preserving Simplified.* Baltimore: The Gas & Electric Company, July 1939.

Honey, Maureen. *Creating Rosie the Riveter: Class, Gender and Propaganda During World War II.* Amherst, Mass.: University of Massachusetts Press, 1984.

Hoopes, Roy. *Americans Remember the Home Front: An Oral Narrative.* New York: Hawthorne Books, 1977.

————. *When the Stars Went to War: Hollywood and World War II.* New York: Random House, 1994.

Kennett, Lee. *For the Duration: The United States Goes to War, Pearl Harbor–1942.* New York: Charles Scribner's Sons, 1985.

Ladies' Home Journal Magazine. January 1940 through December 1945.

Light, Fred Victor. *Recipes for Pressure Saucepan Cooking.* New York: Franklin Press, 1940.

Lindlahr, Victor H. *Successful Salads: How to Make and Use Them During Rationing and Wartime Food Scarcities.* New York: Journal of Living Publishing Co., 1943.

Lingeman, Richard R. *Don't You Know There's a War On?: The American Home Front, 1941–1945.* New York: G. P. Putnam's Sons, 1970.

McCall's Magazine. January 1940 through December 1945.

Mintz, Steven and Susan Kellogg. *Domestic Revolutions: A Social History of American Family Life.* New York: Macmillan, 1988.

National Live Stock and Meat Board. *Victory Meat Extenders: Meat Recipe Book.* Chicago: National Live Stock and Meat Board, 1942.

New York State Bureau of Milk Publicity. *Victory Meal Planner.* Albany: New York State, 1942.

O'Brien, Kenneth Paul, and Lynn Hudson Parsons, eds. *The Home-Front War: World War II and American Society.* Westport, Conn.: Greenwood Press, 1995.

Office of War Information. *Battle Stations for All.* Washington, D.C.: U.S. Government Printing Office, 1943.

O'Neill, William L. *A Democracy at War: America's Fight at Home & Abroad in World War II.* Cambridge, Mass.: Harvard University Press, 1993.

Penny, Prudence. *Coupon Cookery.* Hollywood, Calif.: Murray & Gee, 1943.

Pierce, Anne, ed. *Home Canning for Victory: Pickling, Preserving, Dehydrating.* New York: M. Barrows, 1942.

Procter and Gamble Co. *Recipes for Good Eating,* 1945.

Rupp, Leila. *Mobilizing Women for War: German and American Propaganda, 1939–1945*. Princeton: Princeton University Press, 1978.

Servel, Inc. Peacetime Manufacturers of the Servel Gas Refrigerator. *Eating for Fitness: Home Volunteers Guide to Better Nutrition*, 1943.

Tennessee Department of Agriculture. *Tennessee Home Food Supply Program*. Nashville: State of Tennessee, 1941.

Tuttle, William M., Jr. *Daddy's Gone to War: The Second World War in the Lives of America's Children*. New York: Oxford University Press, 1993.

Ward, Barbara M., ed. *Produce & Conserve, Share & Play Square: The Grocer & the Consumer on the Home-Front Battlefield During World War II*. Portsmouth, N.H.: Strawbery Banke Museum, 1994.

Weatherford, Doris. *American Women and World War II*. New York: Facts on File, 1990.

Welsh, Sarah Francis. *Western Maryland Dairy Cookbook*. Baltimore: Western Maryland Dairy.

Woman's Home Companion Magazine. January 1940 through December 1945.

Index